HARCOURT HORIZONS

Texas

Activity Book

Harcourt

Orlando Austin Chicago New York Toronto London San Diego

Visit *The Learning Site!*
www.harcourtschool.com

Printed in the United States of America

ISBN 0-15-322598-X

19 1421 13 12 11
4500324804

The activities in this book reinforce social studies concepts and skills in **Harcourt Horizons: Texas**. There is one activity for every lesson and skill in the Pupil Edition. Copies of the activity pages appear with answers in the Teacher's Edition. In addition to activities, this book also contains reproductions of the graphic organizers that appear in the chapter reviews in the Pupil Edition. Multiple-choice test preparation pages for student practice are also provided. A blank multiple-choice answer sheet can be found after these content pages.

Contents

·UNIT·

5

·UNIT·

6

Name ______________________________ Date ______________

Multiple-Choice Answer Sheet

Number your answers to match the questions on the test preparation page.

____ Ⓐ Ⓑ Ⓒ Ⓓ	____ Ⓐ Ⓑ Ⓒ Ⓓ	____ Ⓐ Ⓑ Ⓒ Ⓓ
____ Ⓕ Ⓖ Ⓗ Ⓙ	____ Ⓕ Ⓖ Ⓗ Ⓙ	____ Ⓕ Ⓖ Ⓗ Ⓙ
____ Ⓐ Ⓑ Ⓒ Ⓓ	____ Ⓐ Ⓑ Ⓒ Ⓓ	____ Ⓐ Ⓑ Ⓒ Ⓓ
____ Ⓕ Ⓖ Ⓗ Ⓙ	____ Ⓕ Ⓖ Ⓗ Ⓙ	____ Ⓕ Ⓖ Ⓗ Ⓙ
____ Ⓐ Ⓑ Ⓒ Ⓓ	____ Ⓐ Ⓑ Ⓒ Ⓓ	____ Ⓐ Ⓑ Ⓒ Ⓓ
____ Ⓐ Ⓑ Ⓒ Ⓓ	____ Ⓐ Ⓑ Ⓒ Ⓓ	____ Ⓐ Ⓑ Ⓒ Ⓓ
____ Ⓕ Ⓖ Ⓗ Ⓙ	____ Ⓕ Ⓖ Ⓗ Ⓙ	____ Ⓕ Ⓖ Ⓗ Ⓙ
____ Ⓐ Ⓑ Ⓒ Ⓓ	____ Ⓐ Ⓑ Ⓒ Ⓓ	____ Ⓐ Ⓑ Ⓒ Ⓓ
____ Ⓕ Ⓖ Ⓗ Ⓙ	____ Ⓕ Ⓖ Ⓗ Ⓙ	____ Ⓕ Ⓖ Ⓗ Ⓙ
____ Ⓐ Ⓑ Ⓒ Ⓓ	____ Ⓐ Ⓑ Ⓒ Ⓓ	____ Ⓐ Ⓑ Ⓒ Ⓓ
____ Ⓐ Ⓑ Ⓒ Ⓓ	____ Ⓐ Ⓑ Ⓒ Ⓓ	____ Ⓐ Ⓑ Ⓒ Ⓓ
____ Ⓕ Ⓖ Ⓗ Ⓙ	____ Ⓕ Ⓖ Ⓗ Ⓙ	____ Ⓕ Ⓖ Ⓗ Ⓙ
____ Ⓐ Ⓑ Ⓒ Ⓓ	____ Ⓐ Ⓑ Ⓒ Ⓓ	____ Ⓐ Ⓑ Ⓒ Ⓓ
____ Ⓕ Ⓖ Ⓗ Ⓙ	____ Ⓕ Ⓖ Ⓗ Ⓙ	____ Ⓕ Ⓖ Ⓗ Ⓙ
____ Ⓐ Ⓑ Ⓒ Ⓓ	____ Ⓐ Ⓑ Ⓒ Ⓓ	____ Ⓐ Ⓑ Ⓒ Ⓓ
____ Ⓐ Ⓑ Ⓒ Ⓓ	____ Ⓐ Ⓑ Ⓒ Ⓓ	____ Ⓐ Ⓑ Ⓒ Ⓓ
____ Ⓕ Ⓖ Ⓗ Ⓙ	____ Ⓕ Ⓖ Ⓗ Ⓙ	____ Ⓕ Ⓖ Ⓗ Ⓙ
____ Ⓐ Ⓑ Ⓒ Ⓓ	____ Ⓐ Ⓑ Ⓒ Ⓓ	____ Ⓐ Ⓑ Ⓒ Ⓓ
____ Ⓕ Ⓖ Ⓗ Ⓙ	____ Ⓕ Ⓖ Ⓗ Ⓙ	____ Ⓕ Ⓖ Ⓗ Ⓙ
____ Ⓐ Ⓑ Ⓒ Ⓓ	____ Ⓐ Ⓑ Ⓒ Ⓓ	____ Ⓐ Ⓑ Ⓒ Ⓓ

Name ______________________ Date ______________

Compare Primary and Secondary Sources

Directions **Below are two sources, one primary and the other secondary. Both give information about Sam Houston, a Texan who did not want Texas to join other Southern states during the Civil War. Use these sources to answer the questions. Write *Source A* or *Source B* in the space provided.**

Source A: From a speech given by Sam Houston on March 31, 1861

Fellow Citizens: It is not my purpose or desire to address you today upon the great issues now [facing] our common country, but [to] . . . explain the reason why I refuse to [promise to support] the Confederate Government [formed by the Southern states] . . .

The [United States] Constitution . . . and its starry flag are glorious [symbols given] to the South and all sections of our common country by [George] Washington, and all the brave revolutionary soldiers, who fought for and won American Independence. . . .

Source B: Sam Houston

Sam Houston was a hero of the Texan army in the fight against Mexico. He won an important victory and captured the leader of the Mexican army. His efforts helped Texas to win its independence from Mexico.

After the war with Mexico, Houston was elected president of the Republic of Texas. Later, when Texas became a state, Houston served as a senator. He was elected governor in 1859. In 1861, however, he stated in a speech that he was against joining the Confederacy. After that, Houston was removed from the office of governor.

1. Which source is by someone who was there in 1861? ______________
2. Which source was written after the events of 1861? ______________
3. Which source uses the words *I* and *my*? ______________
4. Which source is the secondary source? ______________
5. Which source is the primary source? ______________

Name ______________________ Date ______________

Why Geography Matters

Directions **Use the words in the box below to complete the sentences.**

geography	location
human	physical
interact	regions

1 ______________ is the study of Earth and the people who live on it. There are five themes within geography. One theme is place, which deals with

2 ______________ features of Earth, such as landforms and bodies of

water. Place also deals with 3 ______________ features, such as buildings and roads, which are created by people. Another theme of geography is human-environment interactions, which are the ways in which people

4 ______________ with, or act toward, one another and the land. Movement is another theme. The movement of people, things, and ideas affects the world.

Another theme is 5 ______________, which means the place where

everything is on Earth. The theme of 6 ______________ has to do with areas of Earth whose physical features make them similar to or different from other areas.

Use after reading Introduction, pages 6–7.

Name ______________________ Date ____________

Texas Land and Water

Directions **Use the words in the box to complete the sentences in the paragraphs below.**

Central Plains	mountain ranges
escarpment	natural regions
Great Plains	plain
High Plains	sea level
basins	

Like the United States, Texas is made up of four ________________ ________________, or areas that have the same physical features. If you traveled by car across the state from east to west, you would start in the area known as the Gulf Coastal ________________. Here the land starts very low. Geographers call landforms level with the ocean's surface ________ ________________.

As you travel west, the land begins to rise until you reach the Balcones ________________________________, a long, steep rock wall. The ________________ ________________ region begins and stretches west in rolling hills. This region is a part of the Interior Plains of the United States, but many Texans just call it the Hill Country.

At the Caprock Escarpment you leave the Central Plains and enter the region known as the ____________ ________________. Tall grasses and few trees show you that this area is a part of the ______________ ________________ of the United States. As you continue to travel west on your journey across the state, the land rises even more.

Texas has three ________________________ ________________. One of these includes the state's highest point, Guadalupe Peak. Your trip across Texas is nearly finished when you enter the Mountains and ________________ region. You will know that you have reached the western border of Texas when you see the Rio Grande.

Name ______________________________ Date ______________

MAP AND GLOBE SKILLS

Use an Elevation Map

The map below, like the map on page 33 of your textbook, is an elevation map. The map in your textbook uses color to show elevation. The map below uses symbols to show elevation. To find elevation on the map below, you must know what each symbol stands for. You can find this information in the map key.

The elevations of Texas are like a staircase. The lowest step is made up of the Gulf Coastal Plain. Three other steps rise higher as you travel west through the Central Plains, the High Plains, and finally the Rocky Mountains.

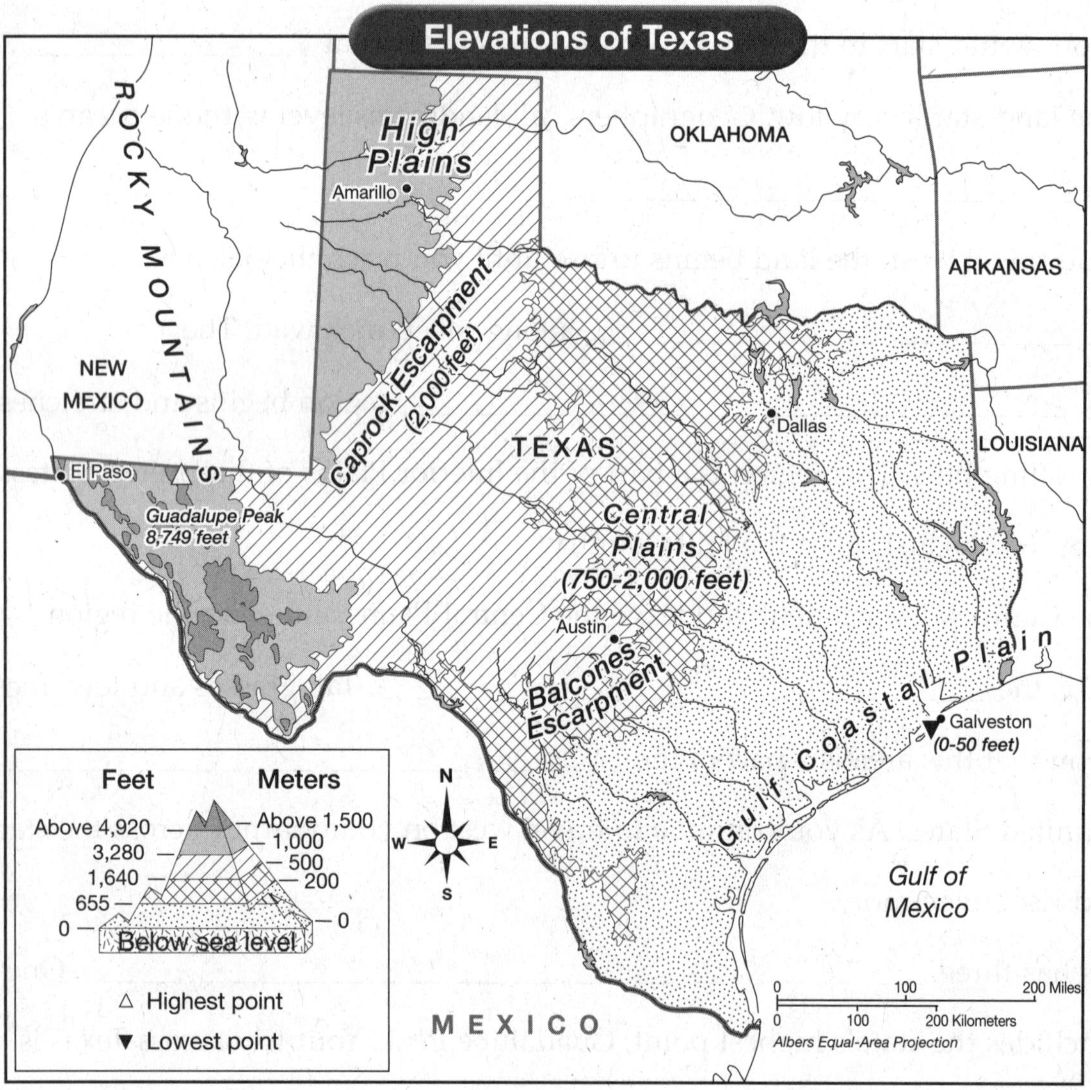

(continued)

Use after reading Chapter 1, Skill Lesson, pages 32–33.

Name ________________________ Date ____________

Directions **Use the map on page 10 to answer the questions below.**

1. Which elevation range covers the largest area in Texas? ____________
2. Which elevation range covers the smallest area in Texas?
____
3. What is the name of the highest point in Texas? ____________
4. What is the elevation of the highest point in Texas? ____________
5. Which city is at the lowest point in Texas? ____________
6. Which city has a higher elevation, Dallas or El Paso? ____________
7. Which city has a lower elevation, Dallas or Austin? ____________
8. What is the elevation range of the Balcones Escarpment?
____
9. Which natural region of Texas has most of the state's lakes?
____
10. In what direction do most rivers flow in Texas? ____________
11. If you could walk in a day from the lowest point in Texas to the highest point, how much higher would you be at the end of the day? ____________
12. If you wanted to live in a city shown on the map with an elevation greater than 3,280 feet, where could you live? ____________

Name ______________________ Date ____________

Texas Climate

Texas temperatures vary widely from place to place and from one time of year to another. The table below shows the average high and low temperatures in January and July for eight cities in Texas.

Average Temperature in Degrees Fahrenheit				
	January		July	
	High	Low	High	Low
Amarillo	49	22	91	66
Abilene	56	31	95	73
Dallas/Fort Worth	54	34	98	75
El Paso	58	30	95	70
Austin	59	39	95	74
Del Rio	63	38	98	74
Houston	62	41	94	73
Brownsville	70	51	93	76

Directions **Use the information about temperatures in these Texas cities to answer the questions below.**

1. Which city has the lowest average temperature in January? ____________
2. Which city has the highest average temperature in January? ____________
3. Compare the January high and low average temperatures in these cities. Which city has the greatest difference between the high and low temperatures?

   ____

4. Compare the July high and low average temperatures in these cities. In which city does the temperature vary the least? ____________
5. Which city's average temperatures appeal to you the most? Why?

   ____

   ____

   ____

Use after reading Chapter 1, Lesson 3, pages 34–37.

Name ______________________________ Date ______________

Texas Plants and Animals

Directions **Draw a line to match the drawing and description of each animal in the left column with its name in the right column.**

	You should be careful not to step on me! When people are nearby, I rattle my tail to warn them not to come closer. You can find me in all parts of Texas. I like warm places and eat small animals such as mice and rats.	**alligator**
	Look for me in grassy areas such as the Texas Panhandle. If I see you near my burrow in the ground, I may bark loudly to warn others. My name might make you think I am a dog, but I am really a kind of squirrel.	**armadillo**
	I live in marshy areas near the Gulf coast. Be careful not to get too close to me, because I can be very dangerous. I sometimes grow to be 12 feet (4 m) long. I use my tail to swim, but I can also use my legs to run fast on the land.	**prairie dog**
	I am a bird that runs along the ground. In fact, I can run as fast as 15 miles (24 km) per hour. I have very long legs so that I can chase my prey or escape from danger. Look for me in the flat, dry areas of southern Texas.	**rattlesnake**
	My burrows are dug with my strong front claws. Bony plates that look like armor cover most of my body. I am the Texas state mammal and live in many different regions throughout the state.	**roadrunner**

Name ______________________ Date ______________

CITIZENSHIP SKILLS

Solve a Problem

Directions **Below are some steps you can use to help you solve a problem. On the lines below each step, write why you think the step is important.**

Step 1 Identify the problem. If it is a big problem, divide it into smaller parts.

____

____

____

Step 2 Think of ideas for solving the problem or each part of the problem.

____

____

____

Step 3 Compare your ideas. Ask yourself what is good and bad about each. Then choose the best idea.

____

____

____

Step 4 Plan how to carry out your idea. Can you do it yourself, or do you need help?

____

____

____

Step 5 Follow your plan, and then think about how well it worked. Did it solve the problem? If not, try other ideas until the problem is solved.

____

____

____

Use after reading Chapter 1, Skill Lesson, pages 42–43.

Name ______________________ Date ____________

The Land of Texas

Directions **Complete this graphic organizer to help you summarize information about the land of Texas.**

KEY POINTS	→	SUMMARY
Lesson 1: Where on Earth is Texas? ______ ______ ______	→	**Summary:** ______ ______ ______ ______
Lesson 2: Texas Land and Water ______ ______ ______	→	**Summary:** ______ ______ ______ ______
Lesson 3: Texas Climate ______ ______ ______	→	**Summary:** ______ ______ ______ ______
Lesson 4: Texas Plants and Animals ______ ______ ______	→	**Summary:** ______ ______ ______ ______

Use after reading Chapter 1, pages 18–43.

CHAPTER 1

Name ______________________ Date __________

Test Preparation

Directions Read each question and choose the best answer. Then fill in the circle for the answer you have chosen. Be sure to fill in the circle completely.

1. Texas is the ______ state in the United States.
   - Ⓐ smallest
   - Ⓑ largest
   - Ⓒ second-largest
   - Ⓓ fifth-largest

2. A natural region located in Texas is the—
   - Ⓕ Gulf Coastal Plain.
   - Ⓖ Rio Grande.
   - Ⓗ South.
   - Ⓙ Pacific Coast.

3. The most precipitation falls in—
   - Ⓐ western Texas.
   - Ⓑ the Panhandle.
   - Ⓒ southern Texas.
   - Ⓓ eastern Texas.

4. Which kind of storm strikes northern Texas in the winter, bringing blasts of freezing air from Canada?
   - Ⓕ hurricane
   - Ⓖ blue norther
   - Ⓗ tornado
   - Ⓙ drought

5. The mesquite plant survives in the hot, dry Mountains and Basins region in western Texas because—
   - Ⓐ its seeds are planted along the highways.
   - Ⓑ its long roots search for water.
   - Ⓒ fields are cleared for planting.
   - Ⓓ marshes drain into the bayous.

Use after reading Chapter 1, pages 18–43.

Name ______________________ Date ____________

Political Regions

Different countries may claim a given area of land over time. When a new country claims an area of land, the political region of the land usually changes, too. A new claim often means a new ruling government. The information below shows how the land that is now Florida changed as a political region over time.

Claims to Land That Is Now Florida

1513 to 1763	Spain
1763 to 1784	Britain
1784 to 1821	Spain
1821 to present	United States

Texas, like Florida and most other states and countries around the world, has changed in a similar way.

Directions **Complete the information below to show how the land that is now Texas has changed as a political region over time.**

Claims to Land That Is Now Texas

1519 to 1821	____________
1821 to 1836	____________
1836 to 1845	____________
1845 to present	____________

Directions **Use the information above to answer these questions.**

1. Which country controlled what is now Texas the longest?

   ____

2. For how many years was Texas part of Mexico? ____________

3. For how many years was Texas an independent country?

   ____

4. When did Texas become part of the United States? ____________

Name ____________________ Date ____________

Population Regions

Directions **Circle the best answer to complete each sentence.**

1. The first people to live in Texas were ______.

   Native Americans   Filipinos   French

2. The population of Texas has grown a great deal because of the arrival of ______.

   tourists   immigrants   astronauts

3. Two important contributions that immigrant groups have made in Texas are ______.

   food and music   cars and holidays   languages and schools

4. Immigrants move to Texas to ______.

   find a better or safer life   listen to music   become astronauts

5. The region of Texas where most people live is the ______.

   Panhandle   mountains   Gulf Coastal Plain

6. In the early years most people in Texas were farmers, but now more Texans live in ______ areas.

   urban   rural   mountainous

(continued)

Name ______________________________ Date ______________

Directions **Imagine that you are an immigrant coming to live in Texas. What is life like in your new home? What do you miss about your homeland? Complete the table below. Then share your ideas with a classmate.**

The country I moved from and language I speak	
Five items I packed in my suitcase	
The new foods I eat	
How my new house is different from my old one	
New things I'm learning	
What I do for fun in my new home	
How life in Texas is different from life in my homeland	
What I like best about my new home	

Name ______________________________ Date ______________

CHART AND GRAPH SKILLS

Use a Line Graph

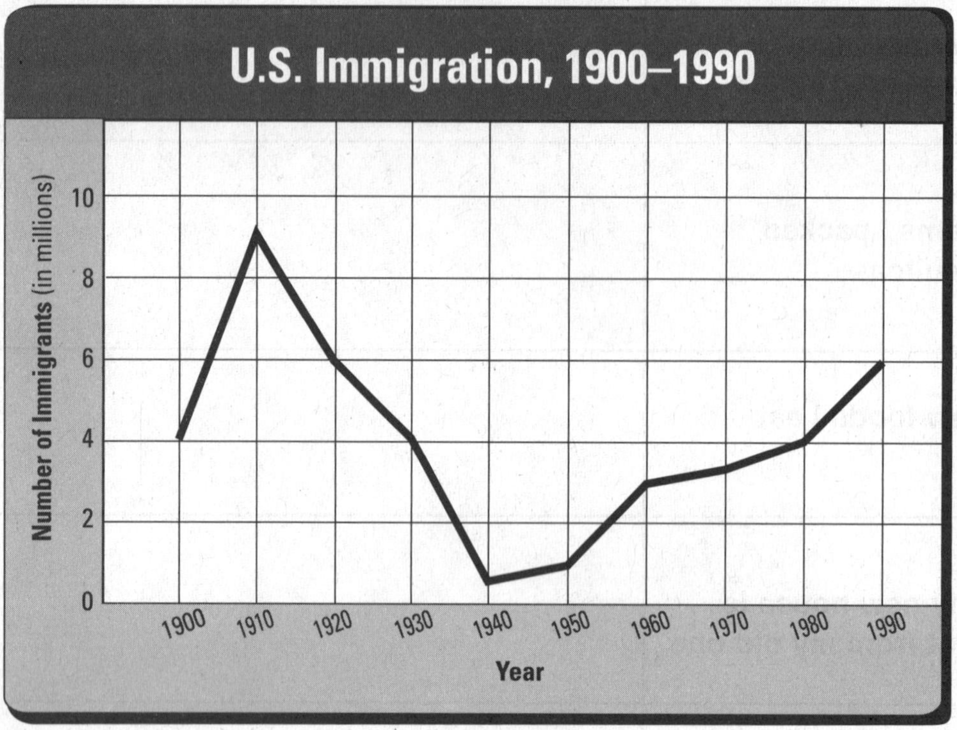

Directions **This line graph shows immigration to the United States from 1900 to 1990. Read the graph to answer the questions below.**

1. About how many immigrants came to the United States in 1980?

   ____

2. What year had the greatest immigration to the United States? ______________

3. In what ten-year period did the smallest number of immigrants come to the United States? ______________________________

4. In what ten-year period did immigration to the United States go from about 4 million to about 9 million a year? ______________________________

5. In what three years was the number of immigrants to the United States about 6 million? ______________________________

 Use after reading Chapter 2, Skill Lesson, pages 58–59.

Name ______________________ Date ____________

Economic Regions

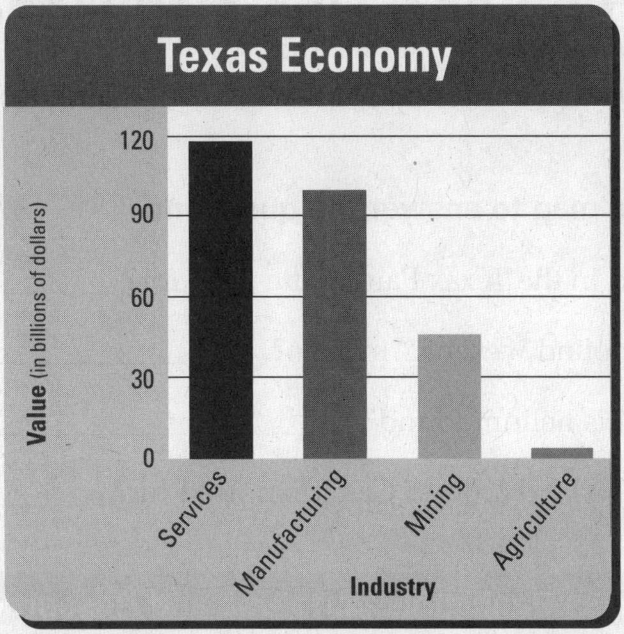

Directions **Use the information in the bar graph to answer the questions.**

1. Which two industries made up most of the Texas economy?

   ____

2. According to the bar graph, which industry made up the smallest part of the Texas economy? ______________________________

3. Which industry made up the largest part? ______________________________

4. Which industry earned more, mining or services?

   ____

5. About how much in dollars did the mining industry add to the Texas economy?

   ____

6. Which industry earned about one-half as much as manufacturing?

   ____

7. About how much more in dollars would the manufacturing industry have to earn to be the largest industry in Texas? ______________________________

Name ________________________________ Date ______________

MAP AND GLOBE SKILLS

Read a Land Use and Resource Map

The map below uses patterns and symbols to show land use and resources in the Texas Panhandle.

Directions **Use the map to answer the questions.**

1. What is most land in the Texas Panhandle used for? ______________
2. What resource is found west of Amarillo? ______________
3. In which counties is helium found? ______________
4. What is most of the land around Canadian used for? ______________

Texas Panhandle Land Use and Resources

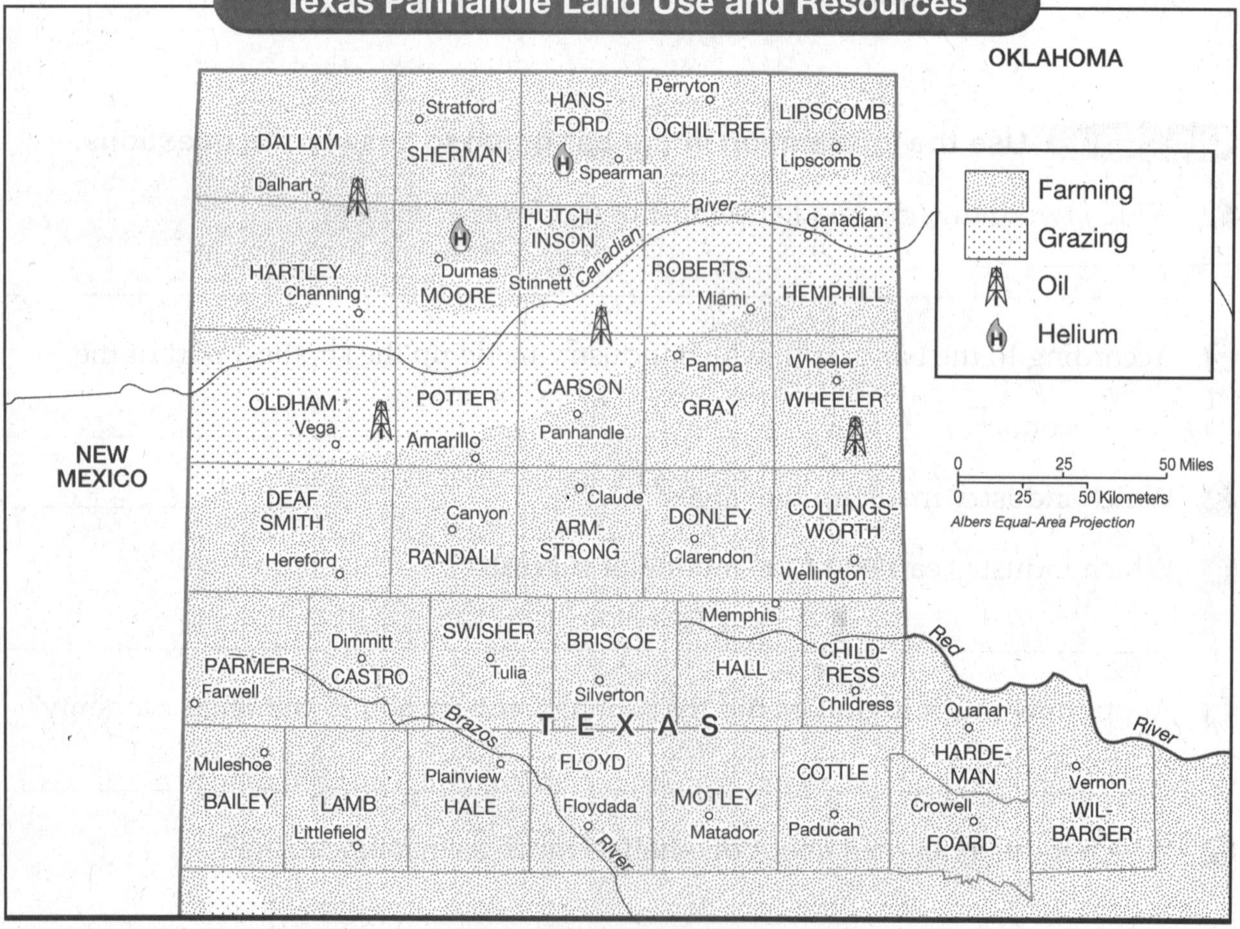

(continued)

Use after reading Chapter 2, Skill Lesson, pages 66–67.

Name ______________________ Date ____________

The map below uses patterns and symbols to show land use and products in the Texas Panhandle. Products are things that are made or raised to be sold.

Directions **Study the map below. Then answer the questions that follow.**

Texas Panhandle Land Use and Products

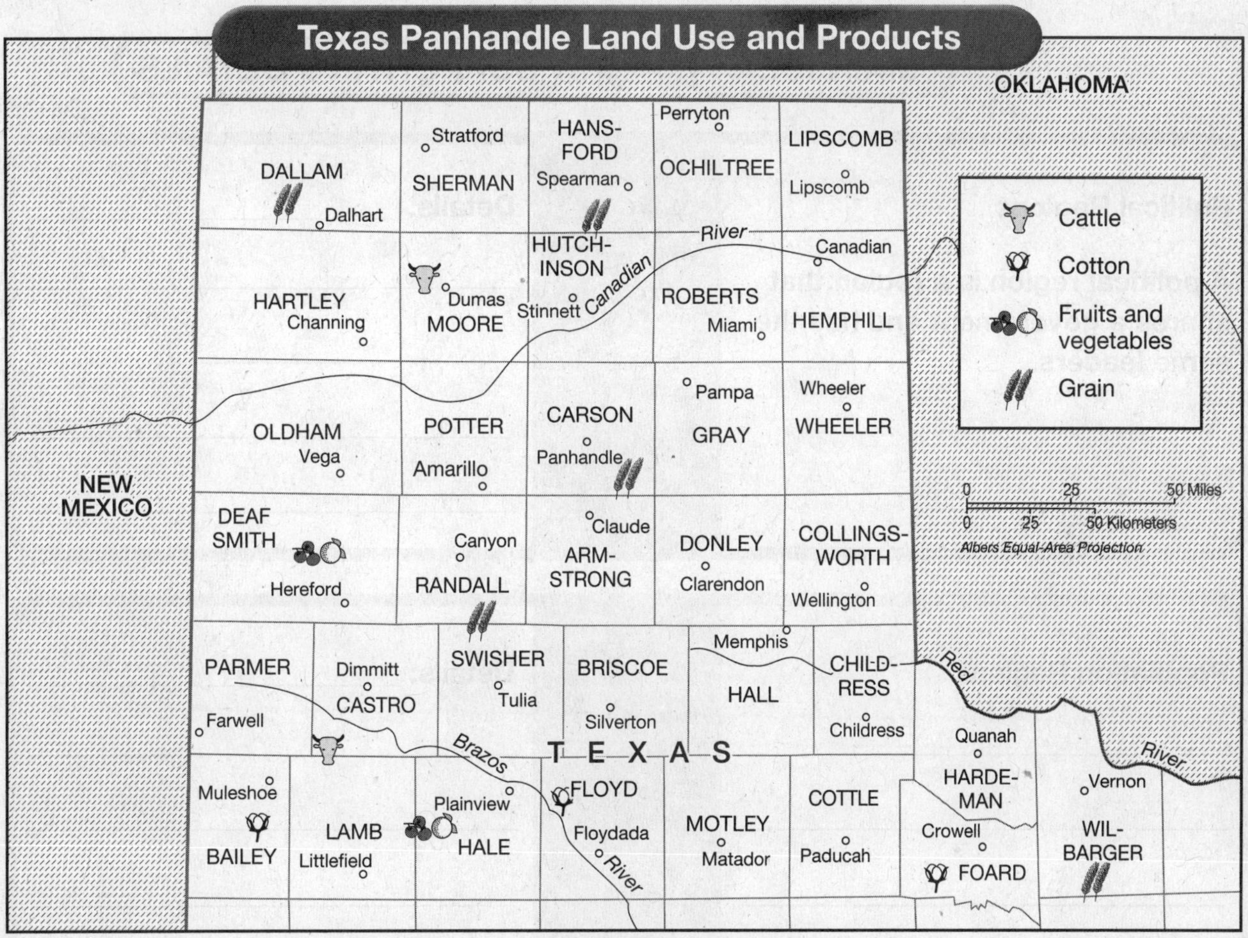

5. What products are found north of the Canadian River?

____

6. What food products are grown on land used for farming in the Texas Panhandle?

____

7. Using both maps, what resources and products are found within 50 miles of Amarillo? ____

8. What product is grown on land in Bailey County? ______________________

Name ________________________ Date ____________

The People of Texas

Directions **Complete this graphic organizer to show that you understand the main ideas about the political, population, and economic regions of Texas.**

MAIN IDEA	→	SUPPORTING DETAILS
Political Regions **A political region is a region that shares a government and has the same leaders.**	→	**Details:** ____________ ____________ ____________ ____________ ____________
Population Regions ____________ ____________ ____________ ____________	→	**Details:** ____________ ____________ ____________ ____________ ____________
Economic Regions ____________ ____________ ____________ ____________	→	**Details:** ____________ ____________ ____________ ____________ ____________

Use after reading Chapter 2, pages 46–67.

· CHAPTER ·

2

Name ______________________ Date ______________

Test Preparation

Directions **Read each question and choose the best answer. Then fill in the circle for the answer you have chosen. Be sure to fill in the circle completely.**

1 Texas shares a national border with which country?

Ⓐ New Mexico
Ⓑ Oklahoma
Ⓒ Arkansas
Ⓓ Mexico

2 Texas, like most other states of the United States, is divided into smaller political regions called—

Ⓕ counties.
Ⓖ settlements.
Ⓗ nations.
Ⓙ provinces.

3 Most Texans live in—

Ⓐ the Panhandle.
Ⓑ urban areas.
Ⓒ West Texas.
Ⓓ rural areas.

4 What two industries do people living in Port Arthur depend upon?

Ⓕ growing crops and raising animals
Ⓖ restaurants and shrimping
Ⓗ fishing and oil
Ⓙ cotton and lumber

5 The use of tools or knowledge to do or make something is called—

Ⓐ industry.
Ⓑ service.
Ⓒ economy.
Ⓓ technology.

Name ______________________ Date ____________

People of the Western Hemisphere

Archaeologists study artifacts, or objects made or used by people in the past. Artifacts are clues that tell about people who lived in a place, or site, long ago. As archaeologists dig through the soil at a site, they may uncover artifacts from people who lived there at different times over many thousands of years. Usually artifacts nearer the surface are more recent. Digging deeper uncovers even older artifacts.

Directions **Imagine that you are an archaeologist digging at a site. First, read the information in the left column about artifacts found at the site. Then, in the right column, list some information about the people whose artifacts were found on each level at this site.**

Level One: 500–2,000 years ago remains of corn, beans, and squash trading beads and feathers pottery made by Aztecs and Incas	**People of Level One** ____________ ____________ ____________
Level Two: 2,500–3,500 years ago remains of permanent shelters evidence of a civilization with a large population	**People of Level Two** ____________ ____________ ____________
Level Three: 4,000–10,000 years ago berry seeds and plant roots bones from small mammals and fish	**People of Level Three** ____________ ____________ ____________
Level Four: 11,000–25,000 years ago deer and camel bones atlatl spear points from mastodon bones	**People of Level Four** ____________ ____________ ____________

Use after reading Chapter 3, Lesson 1, pages 84–89.

Name ______________________ Date ______________

MAP AND GLOBE SKILLS

Use a Cultural Map

The culture map below shows some of the main languages that are spoken today in the Western Hemisphere. You can use this map to learn which language is spoken by most of the people living in a region.

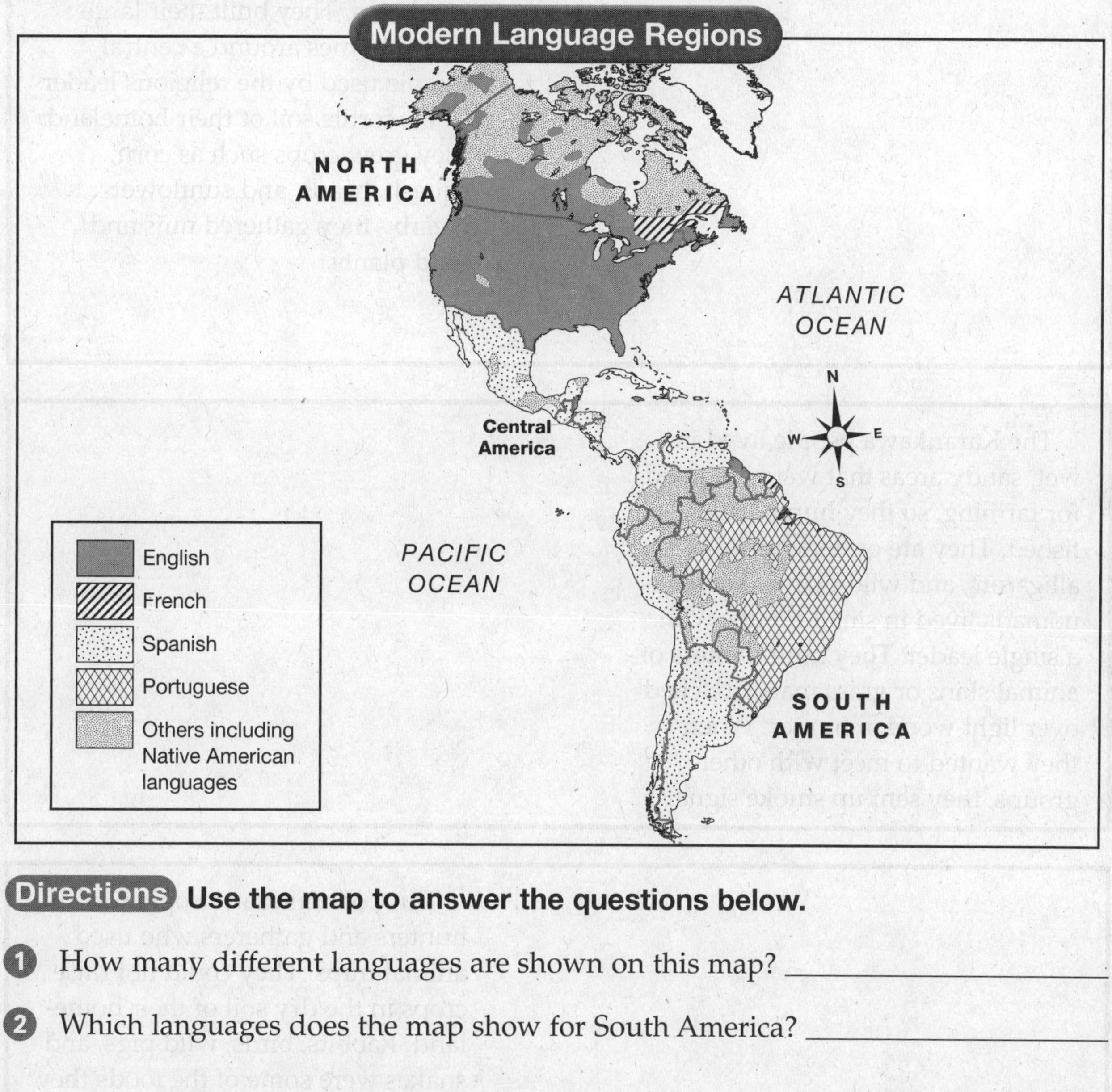

Directions **Use the map to answer the questions below.**

1. How many different languages are shown on this map? ______________
2. Which languages does the map show for South America? ______________
____
3. Which language is most often spoken in Central America? ______________
4. Which languages are spoken in North America? ______________
____

Name ______________________ Date ______________

People of the Coastal Plain

Directions Read the paragraphs below about the three groups of Native Americans that lived in the Texas Gulf Coastal Plain. Then, for each group, draw a picture in the space provided to show a part of its way of life.

The Caddo people hunted deer and bears. They built their large round homes around a central temple used by the religious leader. In the fertile soil of their homeland, they grew crops such as corn, squash, beans, and sunflowers. Nearby they gathered nuts and wild plants.

The Karankawa people lived in wet, sandy areas that were not good for farming, so they hunted and fished. They ate oysters, turtles, alligators, and wild plants. These nomads lived in small groups with a single leader. They built shelters of animal skins or grass mats stretched over light wooden frames. When they wanted to meet with other groups, they sent up smoke signals.

The Coahuiltecan people were hunters and gatherers who used animal traps. They could not raise crops in the dry soil of their homeland. Rabbits, birds, wild pigs, and snakes were some of the foods they ate. They also ate wild plants such as prickly pear cactuses. These nomads lived in small bands, each with a leader known as a shaman.

Use after reading Chapter 3, Lesson 2, pages 92–97.

Name ______________________ Date ______________

People of the Central and High Plains

Directions **Write a story from the point of view of a Comanche boy who has become lost from his tribe while hunting. He is taken into a Tonkawa tribe and adopted. Describe how his new life as a Tonkawa differs from his old life as a Comanche. You may want to include ideas from the list below.**

- food sources
- clothing
- travel
- leadership

Name ______________________________ Date ______________

People of the Mountains and Basins

Directions **Four early Native American groups lived in the Mountains and Basins region of western Texas: the Pueblos, the Jumanos, the Conchos, and the Tiguas. Complete the activities about the four groups.**

1. The houses of the ______________________ were built of adobe bricks, several stories high, and looked similar to modern apartment buildings.
2. The ______________________ split into two groups: those who lived like the Pueblos in settled communities and those who wandered about, hunting and gathering food.
3. The ______________________ grew cotton and wove it into clothing.
4. Because the ______________________ passed down knowledge, traditions, and stories through oral history, they left no written records to explain their mysterious disappearance.
5. The ______________________ were forced to move two times: first by drought and later by fighting with Spanish settlers.
6. The ______________________ lived in dry lands, so they had to use irrigation to water their crops.
7. The ______________________ wandered from New Mexico to eastern Texas, trading for goods such as wooden bows and salt.
8. Each ______________________ family worked its own farm plot, where every family member, including children, had special jobs.

(continued)

 Use after reading Chapter 3, Lesson 4, pages 105–109.

Name ______________________________ Date ______________

Directions **Study the map below. Then answer the questions that follow.**

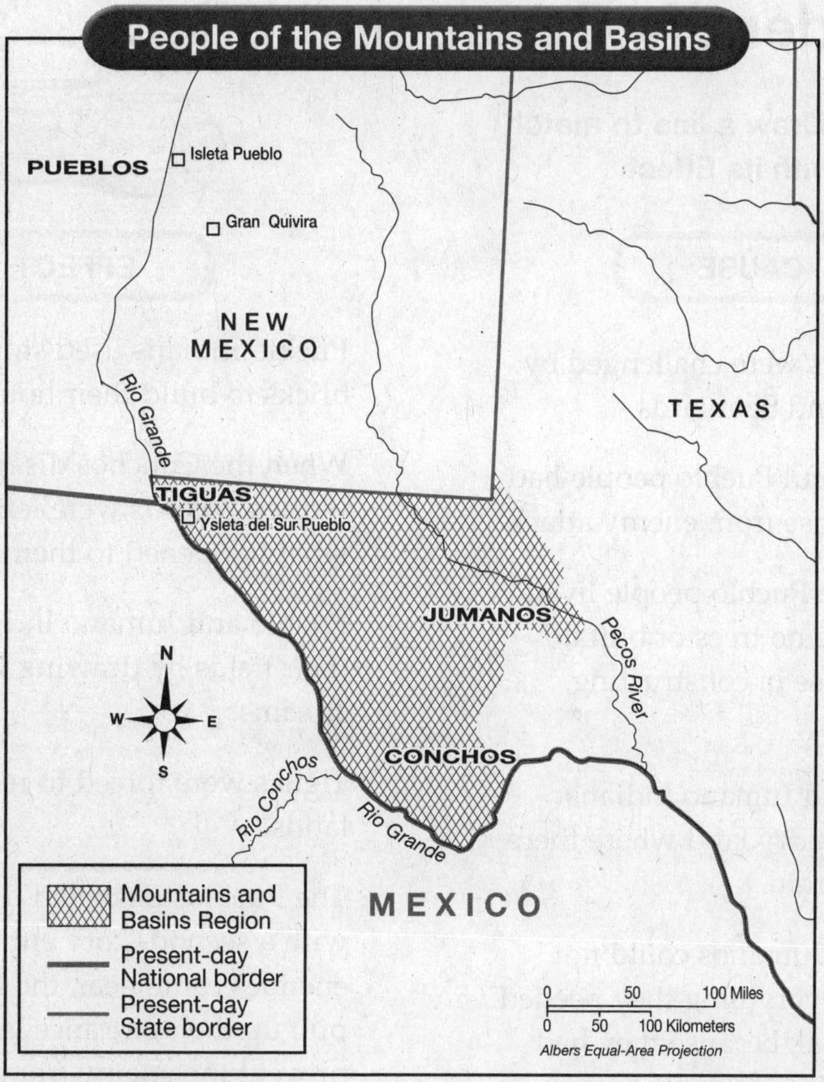

9. What natural resource is near each of the groups on this map?

____

10. Which Native American group lived along the Pecos River?

____

11. Which groups lived along the Rio Grande? ______________________

12. Why do you think all these groups chose to settle where they did?

____

____

Name ______________________ Date ____________

READING SKILLS
Identify Cause and Effect

Directions Draw a line to match each Cause with its Effect.

CAUSE

1. The Tiguas were challenged by drought and Spaniards.
2. The peaceful Pueblo people had little defense from enemy attack.
3. Where the Pueblo people lived, there were no trees or buffalo hides to use in constructing houses.
4. Pueblo and Jumano Indians farmed on dry land where there was little rain.
5. Nomadic Jumanos could not produce everything they needed for survival, because they had no wood for making bows or obsidian stone for making tools.
6. The Conchos kept no written record of their history, passing down stories by word of mouth.
7. The Tigua people, forced from their ancestral homelands, had to work hard to start farms in dry country.

EFFECT

Pueblo Indians used stone or mud bricks to build their houses.

When the Conchos disappeared, no written records were left to tell us what happened to them.

Pueblo and Jumano Indians irrigated their fields by drawing water from streams.

Tiguas were forced to relocate to other lands.

The Pueblos designed their houses with a second-story entrance; when enemies came near, the Pueblos could pull up their entrance ladders to prevent the enemy from entering.

Every Tigua man, woman, and child helped in the farm fields.

Jumano nomads traded with other tribes they met in their travels, obtaining by trade what they couldn't make themselves.

Use after reading Chapter 3, Skill Lesson, pages 110–111.

Name ______________________ Date ____________

The Earliest Texans

Directions Complete this graphic organizer to help you compare and contrast information about the early Native American groups in Texas.

How are they alike? How are they different?

PEOPLE	WHERE IN TEXAS	HOW THEY LIVED
Caddos		
Karankawas		
Coahuiltecans		
Tonkawas		
Lipan Apaches		
Comanches		
Pueblos		
Jumanos		
Conchos		
Tiguas		

CHAPTER 3

Name ______________________ Date ____________

Test Preparation

Directions **Read each question and choose the best answer. Then fill in the circle for the answer you have chosen. Be sure to fill in the circle completely.**

1. Thousands of years ago, a bridge of dry land allowed people to travel between ______ and North America.
   - Ⓐ South America
   - Ⓑ Asia
   - Ⓒ Africa
   - Ⓓ Australia

2. Scientists who find and study things such as weapons and jewelry left by people long ago are called—
   - Ⓕ artifacts.
   - Ⓖ tribes.
   - Ⓗ archaeologists.
   - Ⓙ civilizations.

3. Which Native American tribe kept the soil healthy by planting in a different field each growing season?
   - Ⓐ Caddos
   - Ⓑ Karankawas
   - Ⓒ Coahuiltecans
   - Ⓓ Shamans

4. What resource did Native Americans living in the High Plains and Central Plains depend on to survive?
   - Ⓕ fish
   - Ⓖ buffalo
   - Ⓗ fruits and nuts
   - Ⓙ mustangs

5. What building material did Pueblo Indians make from straw mixed with mud?
   - Ⓐ maize
   - Ⓑ breechcloth
   - Ⓒ jerky
   - Ⓓ adobe

Use after reading Chapter 3, pages 82–111.

Name ______________________ Date ____________

Europeans Explore the Hemisphere

Directions **Look at the three columns below. In the left column are the names of explorers. In the middle column are the names of the countries these explorers sailed from. In the right column are places the explorers sailed to. First, draw a line from the explorer to the country the explorer sailed from. Then, draw a line from that country to the place the explorer sailed to.**

	Explorer	Sailed From	Sailed To
1	Hernando Cortés	Portugal	Mexico
2	Christopher Columbus		Brazil, South America
3	Amerigo Vespucci		Caribbean island of San Salvador
4	Bartolomeu Dias	Spain	southern tip of Africa

Directions **Draw lines on the map from the country each explorer left to the place he sailed to. Label the route with the name of the explorer.**

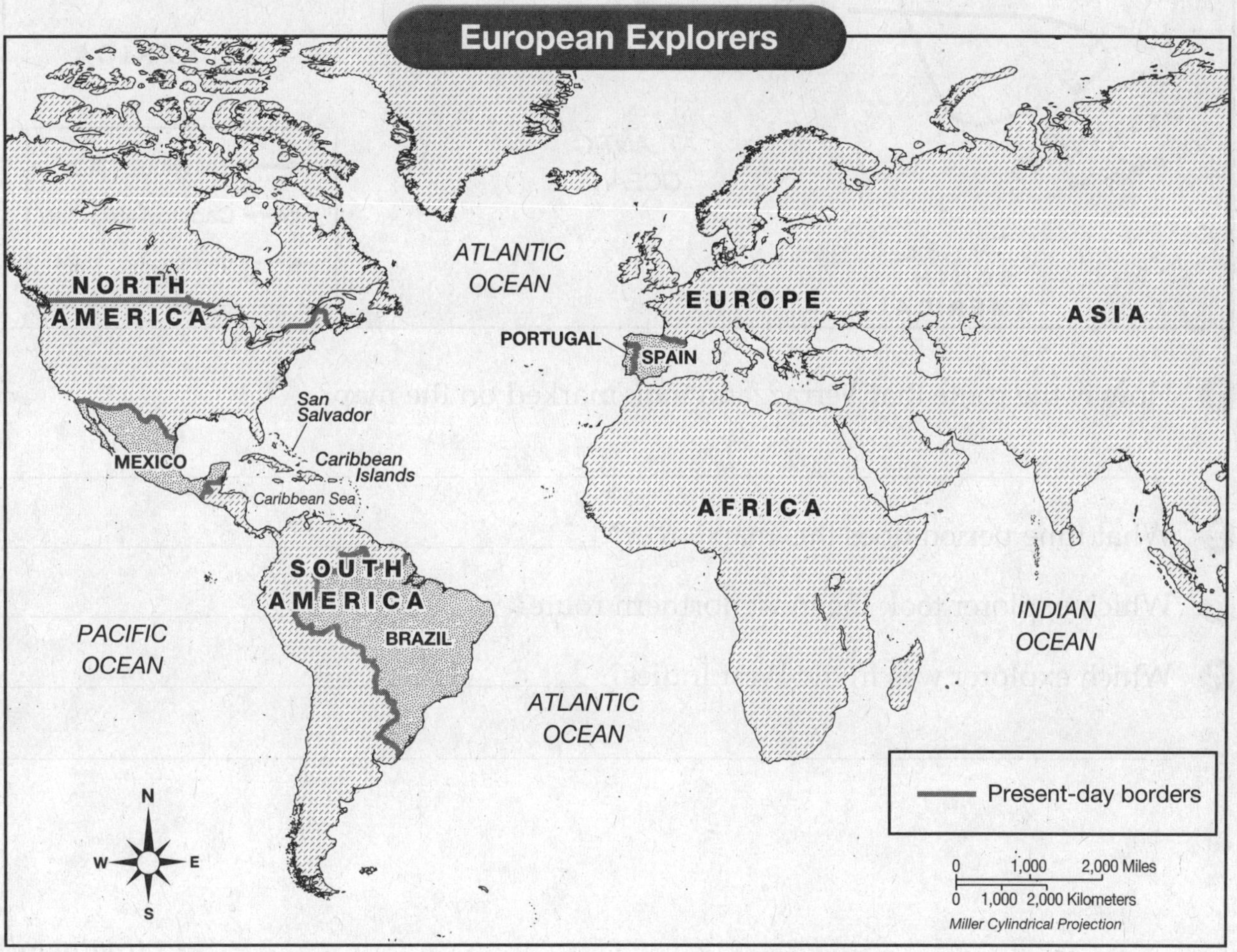

Name ______________________ Date ____________

MAP AND GLOBE SKILLS

Follow Routes on a Historical Map

Directions **Use this historical map to answer the questions below.**

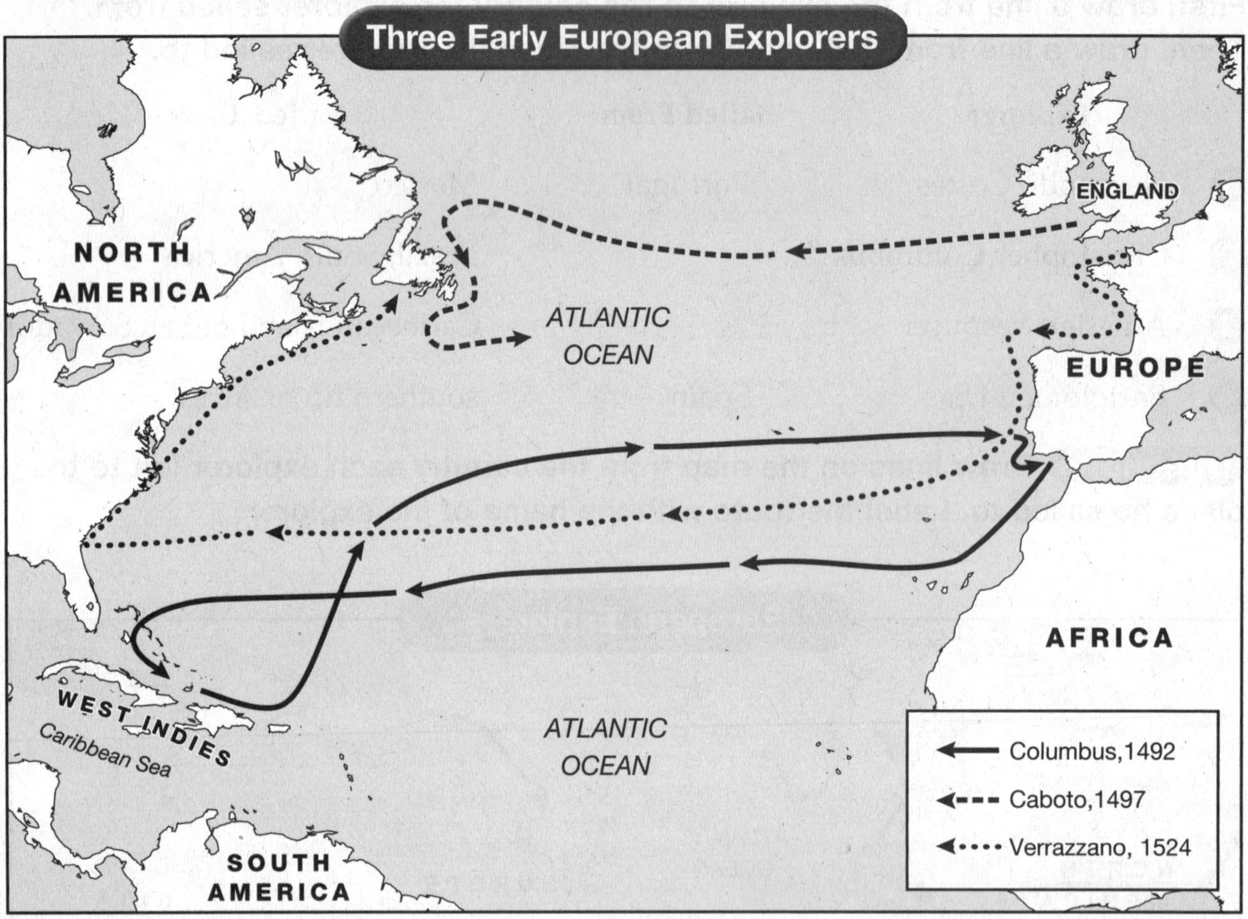

1. How is the route that Verrazzano took marked on the map?

____

2. What time period does this map cover? ______________________

3. Which explorer took the most northern route? ______________________

4. Which explorer was in the West Indies? ______________________

____

(continued)

Use after reading Chapter 4, Skill Lesson, pages 122–123.

Name ______________________ Date ____________

Directions **Use the map on page 36 to answer these questions.**

5. Which of these explorers was the first to travel to the Americas?

____

6. Which ocean did the explorers cross to come to North America?

____

7. Which explorer had the shortest route to North America?

____

8. Look at where Caboto landed and where Columbus landed. How do you think the weather they each experienced might have been different? Why?

____

____

____

9. Describe the route Verrazzano took. ______________________

____

____

____

10. How do you think historians know the explorers' sea routes?

____

____

____

Name ______________________ Date ____________

The Spanish and the French in Texas

Directions **The map below shows some of the places in the South and West visited by French and Spanish explorers. Write the name of each explorer from the list below on the numbered line that matches the place he visited.**

Spanish and French Explorers

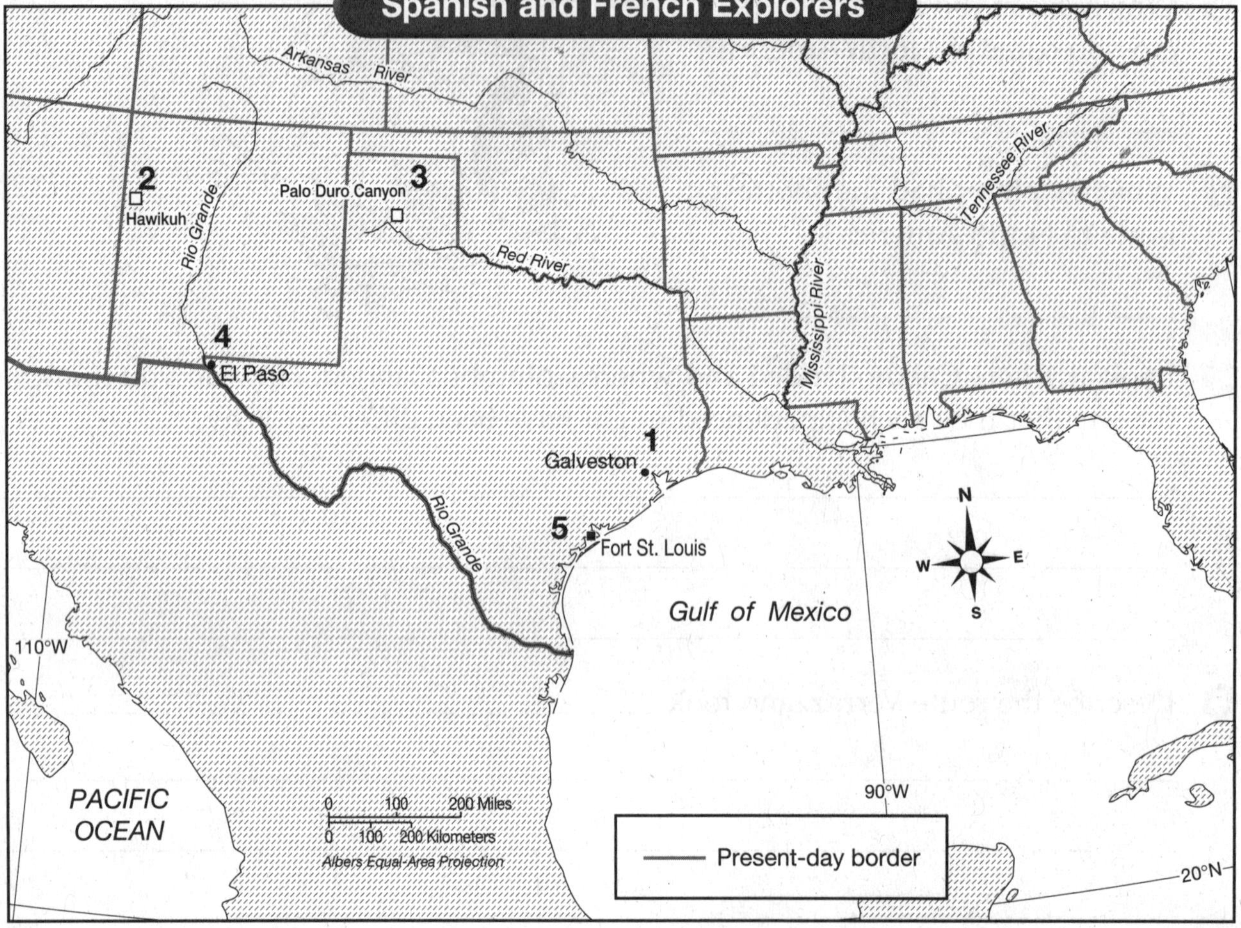

1. ______________________
2. ______________________
3. ______________________
4. ______________________
5. ______________________

Cabeza de Vaca
Coronado
Estéban
La Salle
Oñate

(continued)

Use after reading Chapter 4, Lesson 2, pages 124–129.

Name ______________________________ Date ______________

Directions **Write a paragraph describing the journey of each explorer to the place shown on the map on page 38. Write as if you were the explorer, and tell what you remember most about the experience.**

6 Cabeza de Vaca: ______________________________

____

____

7 Estéban: ______________________________

____

____

8 Coronado: ______________________________

____

____

9 Oñate: ______________________________

____

____

10 La Salle: ______________________________

____

____

Name ______________________ Date ______________

CHART AND GRAPH SKILLS

Read a Time Line

Directions **Notice that the time line in your textbook on pages 130 and 131 covers events in Texas history between 1500 and 1700. The time line below is for the same period in the history of North America. First, examine this time line. Then, answer the questions below.**

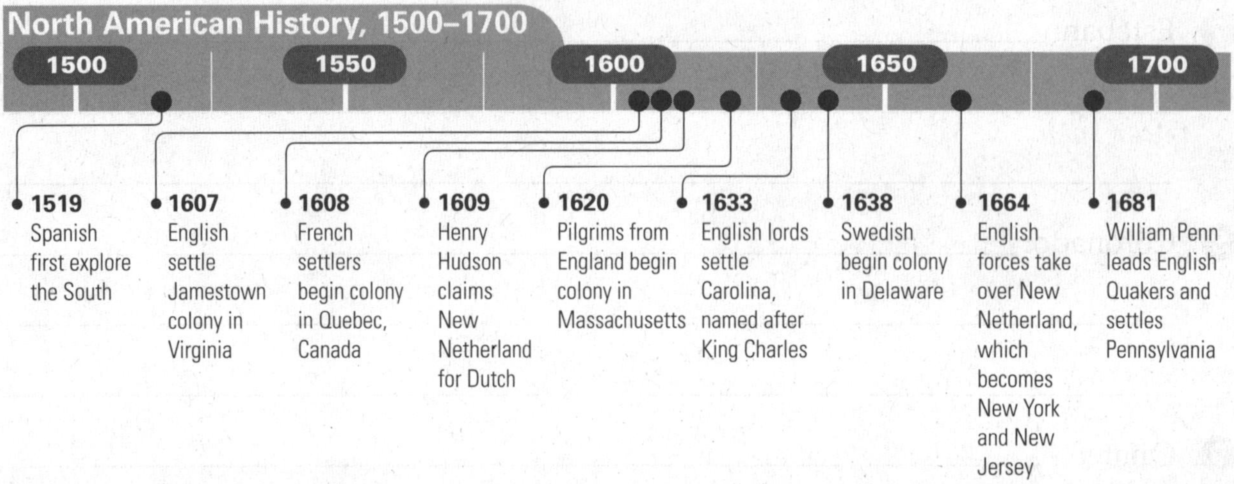

1. How many years does this time line cover? ______________________

2. What is the last event shown on the time line? ______________________

____

3. Which event happened in 1638? ______________________

____

4. In what year was Pennsylvania settled? ______________________

5. In what three years in a row did new colonies begin? ______________________

6. What country founded the most colonies? ______________________

7. Which English colony was settled first? ______________________

8. From which colony were New York and New Jersey formed?

____

Use after reading Chapter 4, Skill Lesson, pages 130–131.

Name ______________________________ Date ______________

Missions, Presidios, and Early Towns

Directions **Fill in the table below with information about missions, presidios, and early towns. Then write a short paragraph in which you compare and contrast them.**

	Mission	Presidio	Early Town
Who built it?			
Why did they build it?			
What kind of buildings and workplaces did it have?			
Who ran it?			
What happened there?			

____

____

____

Name ______________________ Date ____________

Life in the Missions

Directions **Below are some statements that may have been made by people living in Texas missions. Match one of the speakers listed in the box to each statement. Then write the name of that speaker in the space provided.**

Native American farm worker	missionary teacher
missionary farmer	Spanish rancher
Spanish settler	Native American student

1. ______________________ "We get up early here to pray at sunrise. After that I have classes on religion, and then I have breakfast. I am learning how to make soap. When I have learned, I will be able to help the mission."

2. ______________________ "I have a good life here. I have 20,000 head of cattle. We sell meat, milk, leather, and cheese to the settlers around here."

3. ______________________ "I came here to teach the people how to weave and how to build, but my real mission is more important. I came here to teach the people about the true religion."

4. ______________________ "At sunrise the bells ring, but I am already up. I pray to God, and then I get to work farming. We raise maize, melons, pumpkins, squash, and many other crops. Some we use, and some are for the settlers."

5. ______________________ "When we came here, we wanted to make sure we had our home near a mission. That way, we would be sure to get some of the things that we need to live here."

6. ______________________ "I work long hours for the mission farm. I have to do it because there was no food and I do not want to starve. Every day I rise early and plant, weed, and harvest. The plants grow fast because of the water from the ditches we dug to the river."

 Use after reading Chapter 4, Lesson 4, pages 136–139.

Name ______________________ Date ______________

Newcomers Arrive

Directions **Complete this graphic organizer to help you make generalizations about Europeans who came to Texas and other parts of the Western Hemisphere. Try to use words such as *many, some, most,* and *usually* in your generalizations.**

FACTS	→	GENERALIZATION
Lesson 1: Europeans Explore the Hemisphere—Portugal and Spain sent explorers to look for new trade routes to Asia.	→	**Generalization:** ______
Lesson 2: The Spanish and the French in Texas—Spain claimed land in what is now Mexico and the southwestern United States. France claimed land along the Mississippi River.	→	**Generalization:** ______
Lesson 3: Missions, Presidios, and Early Towns—The Spanish built presidios to protect missions. Spain also offered free land, money, and supplies to settlers.	→	**Generalization:** ______
Lesson 4: Life in the Missions—Missionaries tried to convert Indians to the Catholic religion. Native Americans learned new trades from mission priests.	→	**Generalization:** ______

Use after reading Chapter 4, pages 114–139.

Name ____________________ Date __________

Test Preparation

Directions **Read each question and choose the best answer. Then fill in the circle for the answer you have chosen. Be sure to fill in the circle completely.**

1. What small, fast sailing ship allowed Europeans to sail into the wind and travel on rough seas?
   - Ⓐ caravel
   - Ⓑ astrolabe
   - Ⓒ conquistador
   - Ⓓ colony

2. When Columbus landed on the shore of San Salvador, he believed he had reached—
   - Ⓕ the Canary Islands.
   - Ⓖ Spain.
   - Ⓗ the Indies.
   - Ⓙ Portugal.

3. Which Spanish explorer found great treasures among the Aztecs?
   - Ⓐ Columbus
   - Ⓑ Caboto
   - Ⓒ Cortés
   - Ⓓ Vespucci

4. Forts that Spanish soldiers built to protect people living in and near missions were called—
   - Ⓕ missionaries.
   - Ⓖ plazas.
   - Ⓗ vaqueros.
   - Ⓙ presidios.

5. Which religion was brought to Texas by the Spanish about 500 years ago?
   - Ⓐ Jewish
   - Ⓑ Catholic
   - Ⓒ Protestant
   - Ⓓ Islamic

Use after reading Chapter 4, pages 114–139.

Name ______________________ Date ______________

Independence in the Western Hemisphere

Directions **Circle the best answer to complete each sentence.**

1. The war in which the 13 American colonies won independence from Great Britain is called the ______.

   American Revolution   Boston Tea Party   British surrender

2. The ______ states that people deserve "Life, Liberty, and the pursuit of Happiness."

   Magna Carta   Declaration of Independence   Louisiana Purchase

3. The unsettled part of America was called the ______.

   pioneer   frontier   Louisiana Territory

4. The United States wanted the Louisiana Territory in order to ______.

   lower taxes in parts of Texas   control shipping down the Mississippi to the Gulf of Mexico   export perfume to France

5. Until the early 1800s, most of South America and Central America was controlled by ______.

   England   the United States   Spain

6. Simón Bolívar and José de San Martín helped free the Spanish colonies in ______.

   South America   the United States   England

7. Most people in South America in the early 1800s were ______.

   Americans and Texans   Native Americans and mestizos   Portuguese and French

Name ______________________________ Date ______________

CHART AND GRAPH SKILLS

Use Tables to Group Information

The tables on this page show when various states became part of the United States between the years 1790 and 1850.

Table A

State	Year
Alabama	1819
Arkansas	1836
California	1850
Florida	1845
Illinois	1818
Indiana	1816
Iowa	1846
Kentucky	1792
Louisiana	1812
Maine	1820
Michigan	1837
Mississippi	1817
Missouri	1821
Ohio	1803
Rhode Island	1790
Tennessee	1796
Texas	1845
Vermont	1791
Wisconsin	1848

Table B

Year	State
1790	Rhode Island
1791	Vermont
1792	Kentucky
1796	Tennessee
1803	Ohio
1812	Louisiana
1816	Indiana
1817	Mississippi
1818	Illinois
1819	Alabama
1820	Maine
1821	Missouri
1836	Arkansas
1837	Michigan
1845	Texas
1845	Florida
1846	Iowa
1848	Wisconsin
1850	California

(continued)

Use after reading Chapter 5, Skill Lesson, pages 164–165.

Name ______________________ Date ______________

Directions **Use the tables on page 46 to help you complete the activities.**

1. Which table would be better for finding out what year a certain state joined the United States? ______________________

2. Which table would be better for finding out the last state to join the United States between 1790 and 1850? ______________________

3. How many states entered the United States in 1820? ______________________

   Which table is better for finding out this information? ______________________

4. In what year did Vermont become a state? ______________________

   Which table is better for finding out this information? ______________________

5. What states entered the United States in 1845? ______________________

   Which table is better for finding out this information? ______________________

6. Which was first to become a state, Ohio or Iowa? ______________________

   Which table is better for finding out this information? ______________________

7. Which year had the most new states? ______________________

   Which table is better for finding out this information? ______________________

8. Describe in your own words when each table would be more useful.

   ____

   ____

   ____

Name ______________________ Date ____________

Mexican Independence

Directions After reading about Mexican independence, match each event to the year when it occurred. Draw a line from the event to the correct year. Then, in the space to the left of each event, write the numbers 1 to 6 in the order that the events happened.

Event	Date
_____ By this time, groups stopped fighting within Mexico but would later fight again.	1808
_____ Agustín de Iturbide crowned himself Emperor of Mexico.	1819
_____ When a weak king was put on the Spanish throne, the Spanish colony of Mexico used this chance to begin its fight for independence.	1821
_____ Father Miguel Hidalgo y Costilla gave a speech that demanded Spain give equality to all people in Mexico.	1810
_____ Dr. James Long led expeditions into Texas in hopes of driving the Spanish out.	1815
_____ The *Plan de Iguala* made Mexico an independent nation.	1822

(continued)

Use after reading Chapter 5, Lesson 2, pages 166–169.

Name ____________________ Date ____________

Directions **Complete the time line to show the events of Mexican independence listed on page 48. Be sure to include a marker on the time line showing the year of each event and draw a line connecting the year to its event.**

Name ______________________ Date ____________

MAP AND GLOBE SKILLS

Compare Maps of Different Scales

Map A on this page shows land bought by the United States in the Louisiana Purchase. Map B on page 51 shows the route that Zebulon Pike took when he explored areas in and around what is today Texas.

Directions **Study Map A and Map B on pages 50 and 51. Then, answer the questions on pages 50 and 51 to compare the two maps.**

1. Which map shows the Louisiana Purchase? ______________________

2. Which map shows Pike's Route? ______________________

3. What area is included on both maps? ______________________

4. Use your ruler to measure the distance between San Antonio and the Rio Grande on both maps. How far are the two locations apart? Which map is easier to use to find this out? ______________________

Map A: Louisiana Purchase

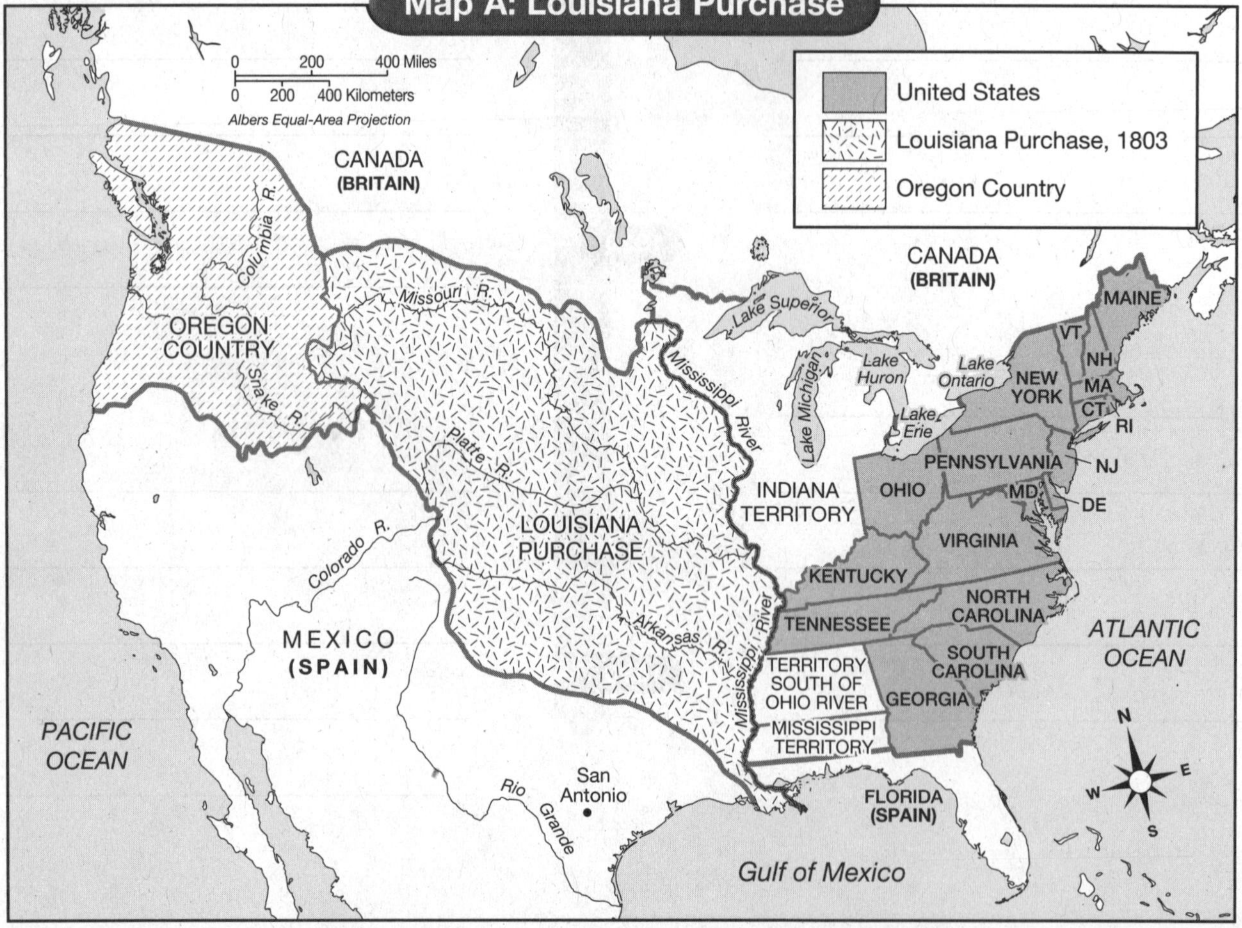

(continued)

 Use after reading Chapter 5, Skill Lesson, pages 170–171.

Name ______________________________ Date ______________

5 Which map shows all of the Colorado River? ______________________________

6 Which map uses the larger scale? ______________________________

7 Which map would be better to use to find out where the Mississippi River flows through the United States? ______________________________

8 Describe what each map is more useful for. ______________________________

____

____

____

____

Map B: Pike's Route

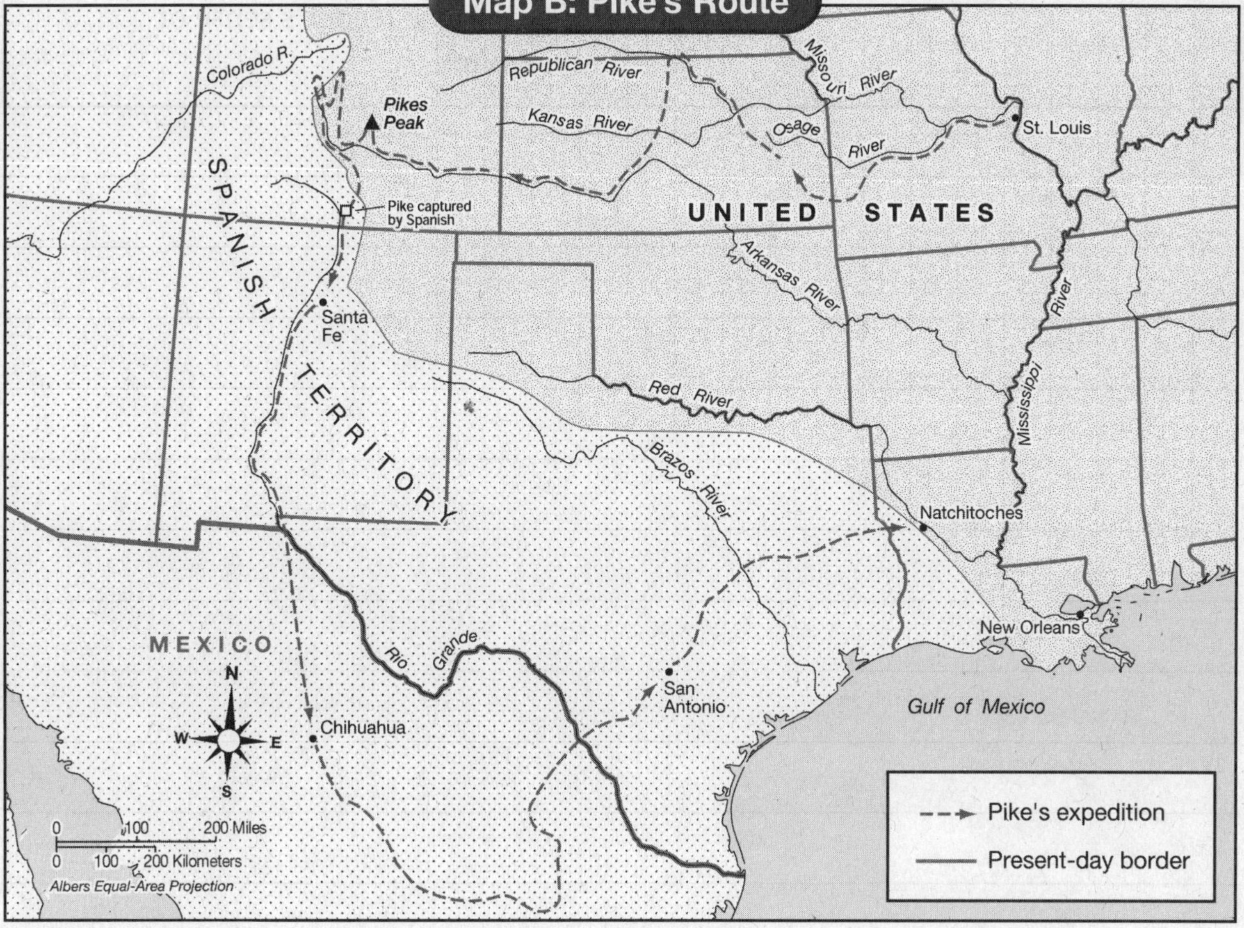

Name ______________________________ Date ______________

The Austins in Texas

Directions **Read the topics below. Then choose one of the activities.**

Topic 1	Topic 2
Write a letter from Jane Long (the "Mother of Texas") to a friend in New York City, describing Jane's new life in the pioneer Texas colony started by Stephen Austin in 1821. **Ideas to consider:** Food was scarce, Indian attacks were common, and neighbors were few and far away. While her husband was away fighting the Spanish, Jane fished and shot birds to feed herself and her little daughter.	Write an advertisement for people living in big cities along the East Coast of the United States. Try to convince them to move to Stephen Austin's new Texas colony. **Ideas to consider:** Be sure to praise the Texas land, and try to make it sound as if life will be easier and better in the new colony than it is in the crowded, noisy cities of the East Coast. Wild horses are free for the roping and taming, and thousands of fertile acres will be given away to each family. Appeal to the reader's sense of adventure!

Use after reading Chapter 5, Lesson 3, pages 172–175.

Name ____________________ Date ____________

Texas Colonies

Directions **Use the clues to complete the crossword puzzle.**

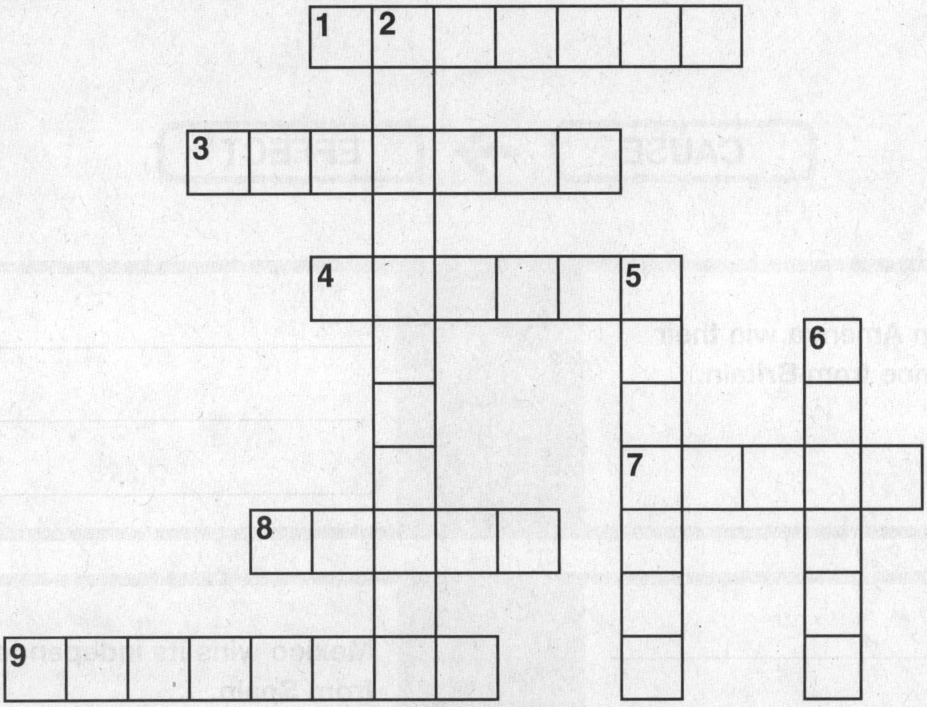

Across

1. Colonists from this country settled the Texas towns of New Braunfels and Fredericksburg.
3. an argument
4. This man had trouble starting his Texas colony in 1825, because the Mexican government had granted him some land that already belonged to someone else.
7. Mexican nickname for an English-speaking settler
8. people from Ireland
9. law-making branch of government

Down

2. men hired by the Mexican government to start colonies in Texas
5. Mexican-born Texans
6. This man, called "Captain Plenty Cows" by the Indians, started a Mexican colony near present-day Victoria.

Name ______________________________ Date ______________

Settlers in North America and Texas

Directions **Complete this graphic organizer to help you understand some of the causes and effects of key events that led to settlement in North America and Texas.**

CAUSE	→	EFFECT
Colonists in America win their independence from Britain.	→	______________________________ ______________________________ ______________________________
______________________________ ______________________________ ______________________________	→	Mexico wins its independence from Spain.
The Mexican government gives land grants to settlers in Texas.	→	______________________________ ______________________________ ______________________________

Use after reading Chapter 5, pages 158–181.

CHAPTER 5

Name ______________________ Date ____________

Test Preparation

Directions **Read each question and choose the best answer. Then fill in the circle for the answer you have chosen. Be sure to fill in the circle completely.**

1. The United States bought the Louisiana Territory in order to control—
   - Ⓐ the 13 colonies.
   - Ⓑ the Rio Grande.
   - Ⓒ the port of New Orleans.
   - Ⓓ Florida.

2. Who helped the country of Venezuela win independence?
   - Ⓕ José de San Martín
   - Ⓖ Napoleon Bonaparte
   - Ⓗ Simón Bolívar
   - Ⓙ the Emperor of France

3. Spain gave up control of Mexico, making it an independent nation, because of the—
   - Ⓐ *Plan de Iguala.*
   - Ⓑ *Grito de Dolores.*
   - Ⓒ empresarios.
   - Ⓓ peninsulares.

4. The first settlers who came to Stephen Austin's colony on the Brazos River were called the—
   - Ⓕ Old Two Hundred.
   - Ⓖ Old Three Hundred.
   - Ⓗ Old Four Hundred.
   - Ⓙ Old Five Hundred.

5. The American settlers of British ancestry who colonized Mexico were known as—
   - Ⓐ Tejanos.
   - Ⓑ Texans.
   - Ⓒ bilinguals.
   - Ⓓ Anglos.

Name ______________________ Date ____________

The Revolution Begins

The Mexican government enacted the Law of April 6, 1830. This made problems between Anglos and Mexicans in Texas even worse. Since the law didn't harm or limit the lives of Mexicans, they did not object. However, Anglos felt as if many of their rights were being taken away.

Directions **In the table below, parts of the Law of April 6, 1830, are written in the left column. Use the spaces in the other columns to write what you think a Mexican or Anglo might say about that part of the law. Try to represent each side fairly, as if you were speaking for a Mexican or Anglo living in Texas in 1830.**

The Law of April 6, 1830	Mexican Point of View	Anglo Point of View
Mexican troops are to be sent to Texas to enforce the law.		The Mexican government is trying to control our lives. We are being denied our basic freedoms.
No new slaves are to be brought into Texas.	You have to obey the laws of your new country and slavery is illegal in Mexico.	
Only Mexican and European settlers may settle in Texas.		You brought us here to help keep Texas safe from Indian attacks. We did what you wanted, and now that we are doing well, you want to control us.
Goods imported from the United States by Texas settlers will have a tax imposed on them.	We need your money in Mexico. You agreed to be Mexican citizens. You should support Mexican businesses and merchants.	

Use after reading Chapter 6, Lesson 1, pages 186–191.

Name ______________________ Date ____________

CITIZENSHIP SKILLS

Resolve Conflicts

Directions **Joy and Phil are having a conflict. Both want to use the playground after lunch. Phil and his friends want to play basketball. Joy and her friends want to play four square. Use the steps on this page to help them resolve their conflict. Try to imagine what each person is thinking.**

1. What is the conflict? ______________________

2. Write what each person wants. ______________________

3. Write how Joy might solve the problem. ______________________

4. Write how Phil might solve the problem. ______________________

5. What compromise can Joy and Phil find to solve the problem? To reach a compromise, they should each be willing to give up something.

Use after reading Chapter 6, Skill Lesson, pages 192–193.

Name ______________________________ Date ______________

Independence Declared

The Texas Declaration of Independence, signed on March 2, 1836, made Texas an independent country. The declaration stated the reasons why Texas wanted to separate from Mexico. Texans felt that the Mexican government was not protecting their freedoms as it should.

Directions **Read the passage below from the Texas Declaration of Independence. Then, in your own words, write what you think the passage means in the space provided.**

Texas Declaration of Independence
When a government has **ceased** to protect the lives, liberty and property of the people, from whom its **legitimate** powers are **derived**, and for . . . whose happiness it was **instituted**, . . . the first law of nature, the right of **self-preservation**, the [most basic] right of the people [is to] . . . take their political affairs into their own hand . . . [and] to abolish such government, and create another [instead, designed to] rescue them from **impending** dangers, and to secure their **welfare** and happiness.

ceased: stopped

legitimate: legal **derived:** brought about

instituted: started

self-preservation: staying alive

impending: threatening to occur soon

welfare: common good

____

____

____

____

____

____

____

(continued)

 Use after reading Chapter 6, Lesson 2, pages 194–199.

Name ______________________ Date __________

Directions Below is a list of Texans that were important in the Texas Revolution. Choose one of these leaders to learn more about. Use the library or Internet to fill in the table below with the information you find. Then use that information to design a monument for your leader that focuses on his or her contribution to the Texas Revolution.

Sam Houston	Stephen F. Austin	Juan Seguin
Lorenzo de Zavala	James Bowie	William B. Travis
Susanna Dickinson	Hendricks Arnold	Dilue Rose Harris

Name of Leader: ______________________

Date and place of birth:	**Monument:**
Date and place of death:	
Role in the Texas Revolution:	

Name ______________________ Date __________

The Fight for Independence

Directions **The events listed below occurred between 1830 and 1836, the years leading up to and including the Texas Revolution. Write the date when each event took place.**

1. ______________ Stephen Austin arrested for treason by Santa Anna and placed in jail
2. ______________ Runaway Scrape begins
3. ______________ Law of April 6, 1830
4. ______________ Santa Anna leads troops to Texas to crush the rebellion
5. ______________ Battle of Gonzales, the first battle of the Texas Revolution
6. ______________ Battle of San Antonio
7. ______________ Constitution of the Republic of Texas accepted by the convention
8. ______________ Sam Houston chosen to become the first president of the Republic of Texas
9. ______________ First fights between Anglo colonists and Mexican troops in Texas
10. ______________ Texas Declaration of Independence signed
11. ______________ Battle of the Alamo
12. ______________ Goliad Massacre
13. ______________ Santa Anna becomes president of Mexico

(continued)

 Use after reading Chapter 6, Lesson 3, pages 200–205.

Name ______________________ Date ______________

Directions **The events on page 60 are not in the correct order. Place the events in order by writing them on the time line below.**

Name ______________________ Date ____________

READING SKILLS

Identify Fact and Opinion

Below is a letter that a young girl in Texas might have written to a friend in the East. Imagine that the writer is the daughter of an American settler in Texas who fought against Santa Anna. The young girl wrote the letter just after the Battle of San Jacinto, when Texans defeated the Mexican army.

Directions **Read the letter below, watching for examples of fact and opinion.**

April 24, 1836

Dear Bobby,

You probably don't know what has happened here, so I thought I would write to tell you. It has been an exciting and difficult time.

1) A few months ago, a Mexican general named Santa Anna came to Texas to fight the Texas settlers to prove that Texas belonged to Mexico. 2) My father had joined Sam Houston's army (in my opinion, Sam Houston is one brave and grand man!) and now Father had to fight. 3) Mother and I got him ready for battle, and he was the handsomest man ever. We waved good-bye to him as he marched off to fight.

Luckily, Father was not in the Alamo when Santa Anna attacked. 4) Santa Anna and his men were nothing but bullies when they kept shooting at the Alamo for 13 days. 5) There were 4,000 Mexican soldiers around the Alamo. 6) There were only about 200 defenders in the fort, and every one of them was killed.

7) Santa Anna is so bigheaded that he probably thought that was the end of the poor Texans. That was not the case! 8) My father, along with the other fearless soldiers of the Texas army, fought back at San Jacinto. 9) The Mexican soldiers were defeated, and I believe they ran just like scared rabbits. 10) The Texans took Santa Anna prisoner. It was a wonderful day.

Yours truly,
Maggie

(continued)

Name ______________________ Date ____________

Directions **For each number below, find the sentence with the same number in the letter on page 62. If a sentence contains only facts, circle *fact*. If a sentence contains both facts and opinions, circle *opinion*. If the sentence contains an opinion, rewrite it to make it a fact.**

1 fact opinion ______________________

2 fact opinion ______________________

3 fact opinion ______________________

4 fact opinion ______________________

5 fact opinion ______________________

6 fact opinion ______________________

7 fact opinion ______________________

8 fact opinion ______________________

9 fact opinion ______________________

10 fact opinion ______________________

Name ______________________ Date ____________

Independence Won

The fight for Texas independence was difficult for both Texans and Mexicans. The final battle was at San Jacinto, on April 21, 1836. Only two Texans were killed in the battle. The Mexican army lost about 600 men and the rest were forced to surrender. The Texans had three main advantages in the battle. They were well rested. They were also first to arrive at the battlefield, which allowed them to choose the best location for their troops. Finally, the Texas leader, Sam Houston, planned a good strategy to win that took the Mexicans by complete surprise. This important battle lasted only 18 minutes.

Directions **Use the map on page 65 to complete the activities below.**

1. In which grid box was the Texan Camp located? ______________
2. In which grid box was the Mexican Camp located? ______________
3. The Texan army took over Lynch's Ferry to keep the Mexican army from escaping. In which grid box was the ferry located? ______________
4. Sam Houston ordered the Texan cavalry to stay hidden in the trees near Buffalo Bayou. Place an X on the map where the cavalry may have hidden.
5. Houston lined up cannons and soldiers in front of the marshlands northeast of the Texan Camp to wait for the battle. Place two lines on the map where the Texan army may have waited.
6. While the Mexicans rested, the Texan army moved quietly towards the Mexican Camp. Draw an arrow on the map showing which way the Texans moved.
7. When the battle started, Houston ordered the cavalry to move south behind the Mexican Camp to keep the Mexicans from escaping. Draw a dotted line on the map to show where the cavalry went.
8. The Texans attacked the Mexican Camp at 3:30 in the afternoon. Because they were surprised, the Mexican soldiers could not defend themselves. Draw a circle around the Mexican Camp showing where the Texans won the Battle of San Jacinto.

(continued)

Name ______________________ Date ______________

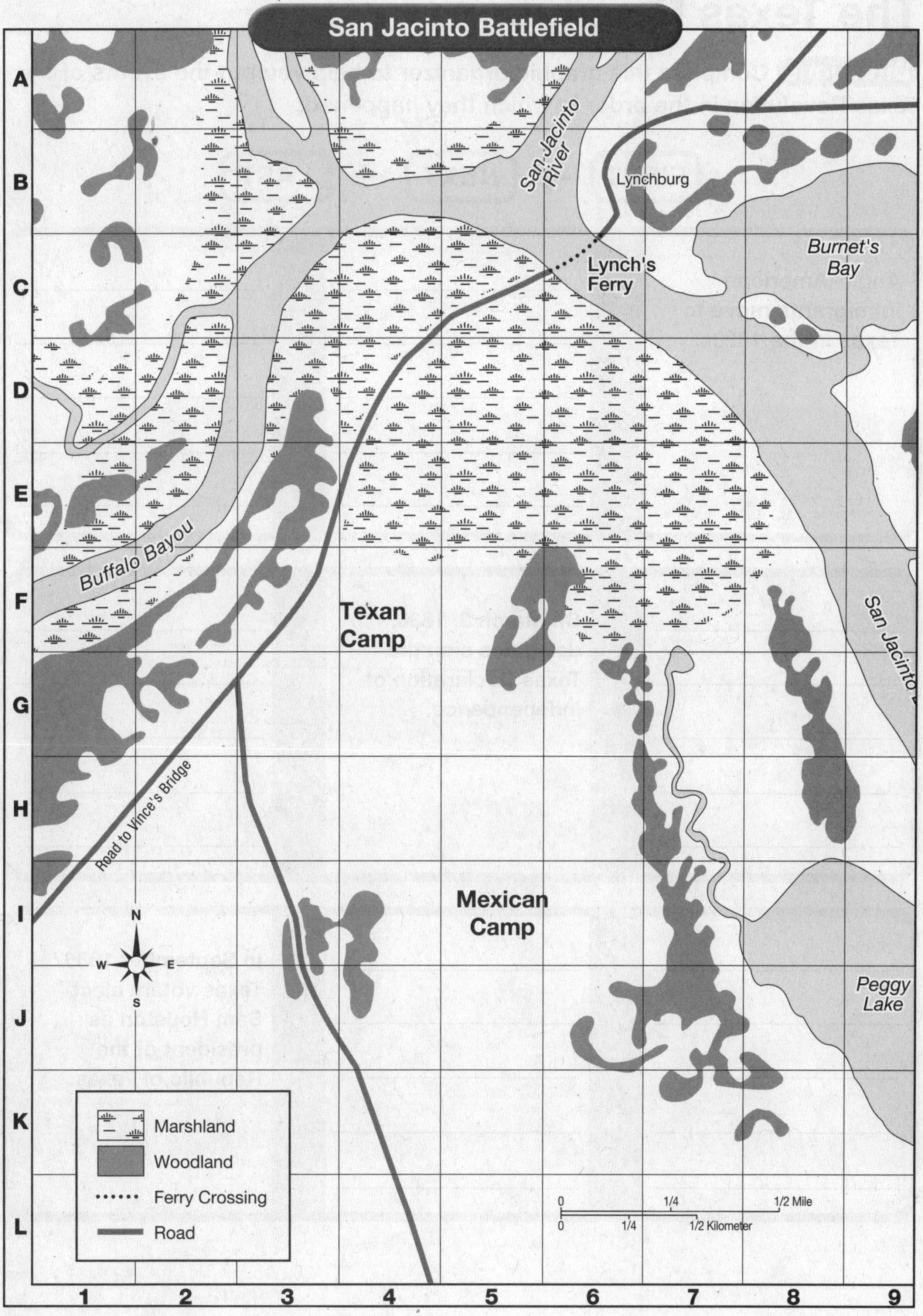
San Jacinto Battlefield
A
B
C
D
E
F
G
H
I
J
K
L
1
2
3
4
5
6
7
8
9
San Jacinto River
Lynchburg
Burnet's Bay
Lynch's Ferry
Buffalo Bayou
Texan Camp
San Jacinto
Road to Vince's Bridge
Mexican Camp
Peggy Lake
N
W
E
S
Marshland
Woodland
Ferry Crossing
Road
0
1/4
1/2 Mile
0
1/4
1/2 Kilometer

Name ______________________ Date ______________

The Texas Revolution

Directions **Complete this graphic organizer to help you put the events of the Texas Revolution in the order in which they happened.**

FIRST → NEXT → LAST

Anglo-American immigrants move to Texas in the 1820s. →	______________ →	______________
______________ →	**On March 2, 1836, delegates sign the Texas Declaration of Independence.** →	______________
______________ →	______________ →	**In September 1836, Texas voters elect Sam Houston as president of the Republic of Texas.**

 Use after reading Chapter 6, pages 184–211.

Name ______________________ Date __________

Test Preparation

Directions **Read each question and choose the best answer. Then fill in the circle for the answer you have chosen. Be sure to fill in the circle completely.**

1. The Law of April 6, 1830, did not allow the settlers to—
   - Ⓐ practice the Catholic religion.
   - Ⓑ pay taxes.
   - Ⓒ bring more slaves to Texas.
   - Ⓓ learn to speak Spanish.

2. Texans decided to declare independence from Mexico during—
   - Ⓕ the Convention of 1836.
   - Ⓖ the Fredonia Rebellion.
   - Ⓗ the Battle of San Jacinto.
   - Ⓙ the Texas Revolution.

3. Who was captured during the Battle of San Jacinto?
   - Ⓐ Sam Houston
   - Ⓑ Susanna Dickinson
   - Ⓒ Lorenzo de Zavala
   - Ⓓ Santa Anna

4. In September, 1836, Sam Houston was elected as the first ______ of the Republic of Texas.
   - Ⓕ senator
   - Ⓖ president
   - Ⓗ chairman
   - Ⓙ general

5. During the Battle of San Jacinto, Mirabeau Lamar led—
   - Ⓐ the Texas navy.
   - Ⓑ the Republic of Texas.
   - Ⓒ the Texas cavalry.
   - Ⓓ the Fredonia Rebellion.

Name ________________________ Date ____________

The Republic of Texas

During the years in which Texas was an independent republic, the young country faced many problems. The three presidents of the Texas Republic offered different solutions to these problems.

Directions **Below is a list of some problems the Texas Republic faced. Think about how each president of Texas tried to solve these problems. List their solutions in the table below.**

Problems	Solutions
Texas had a huge debt from its war with Mexico.	
Mexican soldiers continued to attack Texans.	
Columbia was too crowded, and didn't make a good capital.	
Many Texans wanted the land that the Cherokees were living on.	

Use after reading Chapter 7, Lesson 1, pages 228–233.

Name ______________________ Date ____________

Texas Statehood

Directions **Complete each sentence with an appropriate word or phrase. Note that some sentences have more than one blank.**

1. Many people in the United States and most of the people in Texas agreed that Texas should ______________________ because that might make the United States ______________________.

2. Some United States citizens thought that adding a country as a state went against the ______________________.

3. The Southern states wanted Texas to join the United States since Texas allowed ______________________. Adding Texas might give the Southern states more power in the ______________________.

4. Some United States citizens feared that if Texas became a state there would be a war with ______________________.

5. Mexico did not want Texas to become a state. Mexico feared that the United States would then become even ______________________.

6. Slavery was not allowed in the ______________________, located in the North.

7. Two foreign countries, ______________________ and ______________________, did not want Texas to become a state.

8. The ______________________ states did not want Texas to become a state because they feared Southern states would be too powerful.

9. People opposed to slavery, known as ______________________, did not want to add another slave state to the United States.

Name ______________________________ Date ______________

CITIZENSHIP SKILLS

Make a Thoughtful Decision

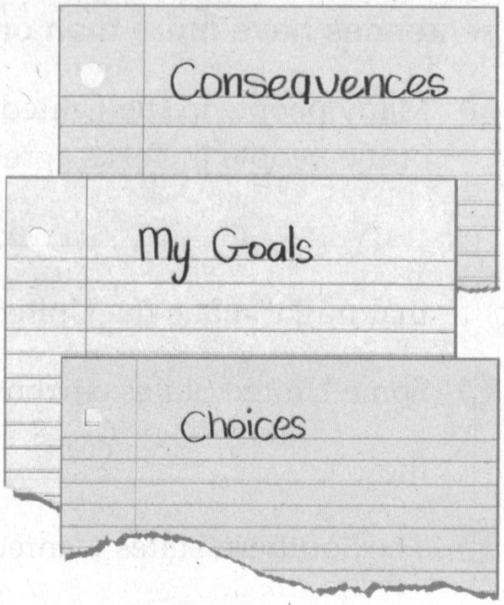

Directions **Imagine that you have a choice to make. Your goal is to have a great birthday party, but your parents have told you that they cannot spend much money on a birthday party this year.**

Here are your choices: you could invite all your friends and have a party at home; you could invite just a few friends and take them to an amusement park. Use this page to help you make a decision.

1. What are the good and bad consequences of having a party at home and inviting all your friends?

   Good: ______________________________

   Bad: ______________________________

2. What are the good and bad consequences of having a party with a few friends at an amusement park?

   Good: ______________________________

   Bad: ______________________________

3. Which choice will have the best consequences? Explain why.

   ____

   ____

4. Could your choice have bad consequences you have not thought of? What might they be? ______________________________

   ____

5. Based on your answer, do you want to change your choice? Why did you make your final choice? ______________________________

   ____

Use after reading Chapter 7, Skill Lesson, pages 240–241.

Name ______________________ Date ______________

The War with Mexico

Directions **Use the clues below to complete the crossword puzzle.**

Across

1. A ______ is land given to another country.
3. The Mexicans and Americans signed a ______ at Guadalupe Hidalgo.
5. The leaders of Mexico were angered by Texas ______.
7. Ben McCulloch was a Texas ______.
8. General Winfield ______ and his troops captured Mexico City.

Down

1. Polk asked ______ to declare war on Mexico.
2. After the loss of Mexico City, ______ stepped down as president of Mexico.
4. James ______ was the President of the United States during the war with Mexico.
6. General Zachary ______ led the troops into Mexico in 1846.

Name ______________________ Date ____________

MAP AND GLOBE SKILLS

Compare Historical Maps

The maps on pages 72 and 73 show the United States at two different times. Map A shows the United States in 1803, when the Louisiana Purchase was made. Map B shows the United States in 1848, as the United States continued its expansion.

Directions **Use the maps on pages 72 and 73 to complete the activities.**

1. What area on the map grew from 1803 to 1848? ______________________

____

2. In the 1848 map, what makes up what was Spanish Territory in 1803?

____

3. What happened to the ownership of Florida from 1803 to 1848?

____

Map A: United States in 1803

(continued)

Use after reading Chapter 7, Skill Lesson, pages 246–247.

Name ______________________ Date ______________

4 How did the Oregon Country change from 1803 to 1848?

____

5 What happened to the northern border of the Louisiana Purchase from 1803 to 1848? ____

6 About how much of what was the United States in 1848 was claimed by Spain in 1803? ____

7 Describe how the land of the United States changed from 1803 to 1848.

____

____

____

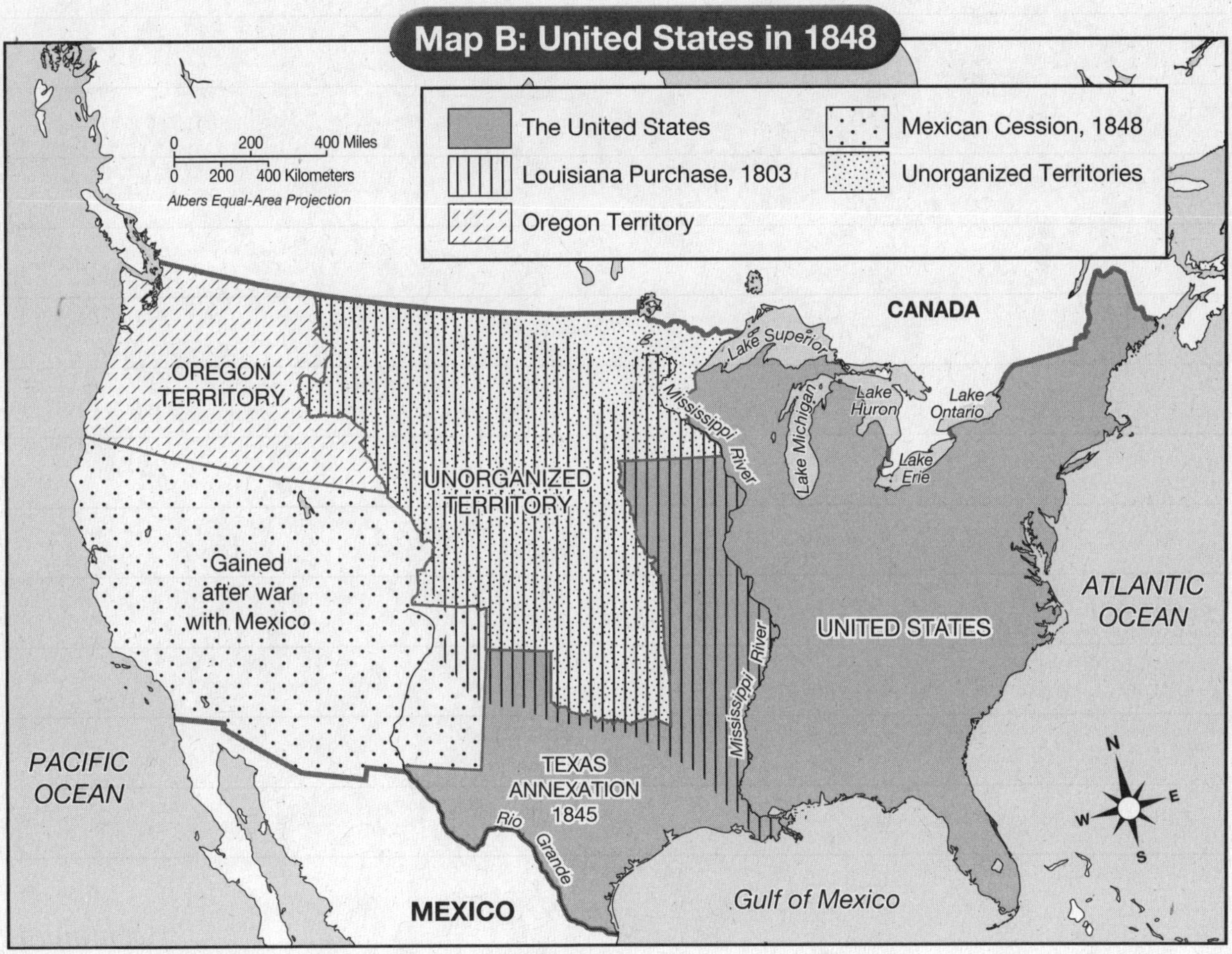

Name ______________________ Date ____________

Texas Grows

Quilt designs can show what pioneer life was like in Texas and other frontier states. Each small quilt block had a design on it that represented something about the daily life of the pioneers. A quilt often told a story or kept a record of the life of the pioneer who stitched it together.

Directions **Look carefully at the quilt blocks on page 75. The names describe what each represents. Choose at least five designs to tell a story about the life of a pioneer in Texas. Write your story below.**

(continued)

Use after reading Chapter 7, Lesson 4, pages 248–253.

Name ______________________________ Date ______________

Indian Trail

Texas Ranger's Badge

Log Cabin

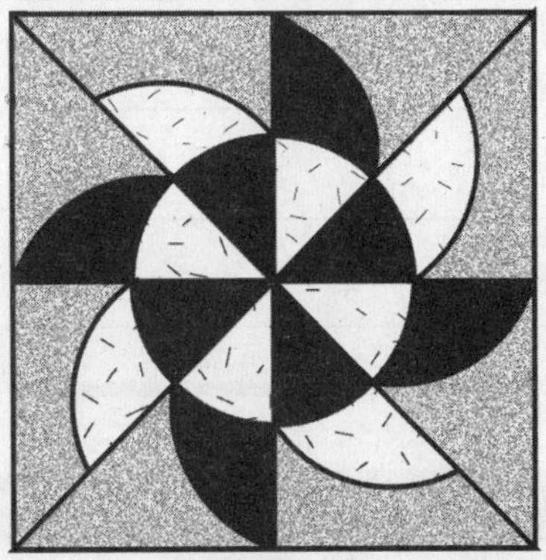
Pig Pen

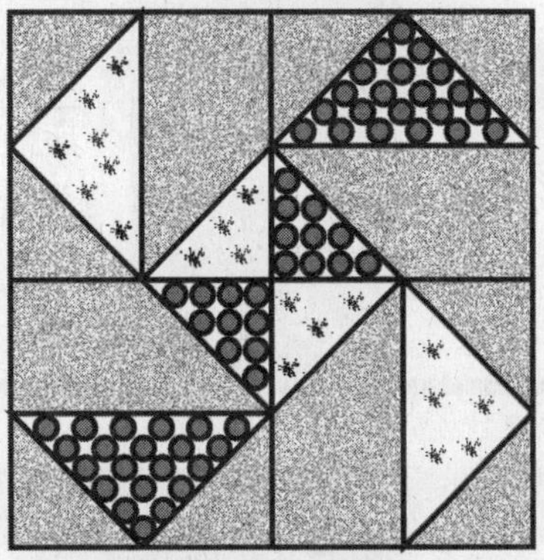
Next Door Neighbor

Tall Pine Tree

Texas Cactus Basket

Goose in the Pond

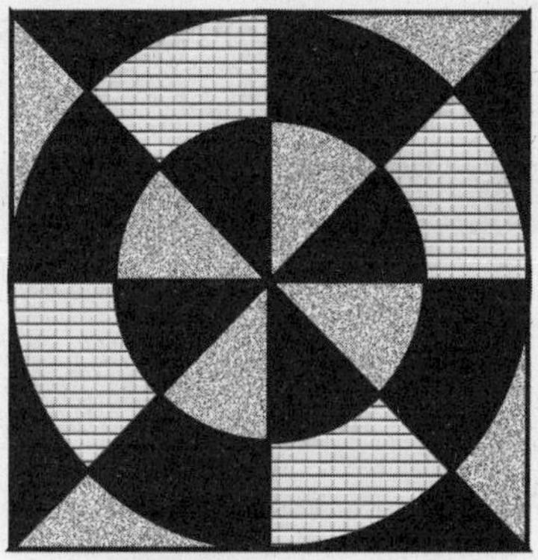
Whirling Dust Storm

Grandmother's Fan

Bear's Paw

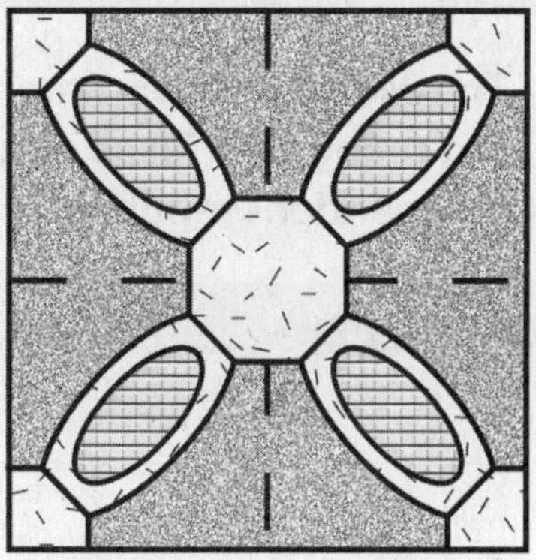
Texas Teardrops

Name ______________________ Date ____________

From Republic to Statehood

Directions **Complete this graphic organizer to help you make some inferences about Texas as a republic and a state.**

FACT		INFERENCE
Leaders of the Republic of Texas faced many new problems.	→	______________________
EXPERIENCE		______________________
Leaders often have differences of opinion.	→	______________________

FACT		INFERENCE
Many Texans wanted the republic to join the United States.	→	______________________
EXPERIENCE		______________________
______________________	→	______________________

FACT		INFERENCE
The Mexican government did not recognize Texas as an independent republic.	→	______________________
EXPERIENCE		______________________
______________________	→	______________________

Use after reading Chapter 7, pages 226–253.

CHAPTER 7

Name ______________________ Date __________

Test Preparation

Directions **Read each question and choose the best answer. Then fill in the circle for the answer you have chosen. Be sure to fill in the circle completely.**

1. A person who is a member of a country, a state, a city, or a town is called a—
   - Ⓐ redback.
   - Ⓑ colonist.
   - Ⓒ citizen.
   - Ⓓ republic.

2. The Archives War started because people worried that Sam Houston would move the capital of Texas from—
   - Ⓕ Houston.
   - Ⓖ Austin.
   - Ⓗ Columbia.
   - Ⓙ Plum Creek.

3. What agreement gave New Mexico, Arizona, California, and parts of Colorado, Nevada, and Utah to the United States?
   - Ⓐ Mexican Cession
   - Ⓑ Texas Declaration of Independence
   - Ⓒ Manifest Destiny
   - Ⓓ Texas Constitution of 1845

4. Newcomers to Texas between the 1830s and 1860s came mostly from which states?
   - Ⓕ Northern
   - Ⓖ Eastern
   - Ⓗ Western
   - Ⓙ Southern

5. In 1850 most Texans lived—
   - Ⓐ in small towns.
   - Ⓑ in large towns.
   - Ⓒ on farms in the western part of the state.
   - Ⓓ on farms in rural areas.

Name ______________________ Date ______________

Texas Plantations

A plantation was like a small town. Like a Spanish hacienda, a plantation was mostly self-sufficient. It had many houses and buildings. Planters grew food, and skilled workers produced many needed goods.

Directions **Look at the illustration of a Texas plantation below and answer the following questions.**

A Texas Plantation

1. Why do you think a plantation needed to be self-sufficient?

____

2. Why were many plantations located next to rivers? ______________

____

3. What was the major cash crop at most Texas plantations? ______________

4. Why do you think the plantation manager's house was located between the main house and the slave quarters? ______________

____

5. What did Eli Whitney invent that made harvesting cotton quicker?

____

Use after reading Chapter 8, Lesson 1, pages 258–262.

Name ______________________ Date __________

CHART AND GRAPH SKILLS

Read a Double-Bar Graph

Directions **Use this double-bar graph to answer the questions below.**

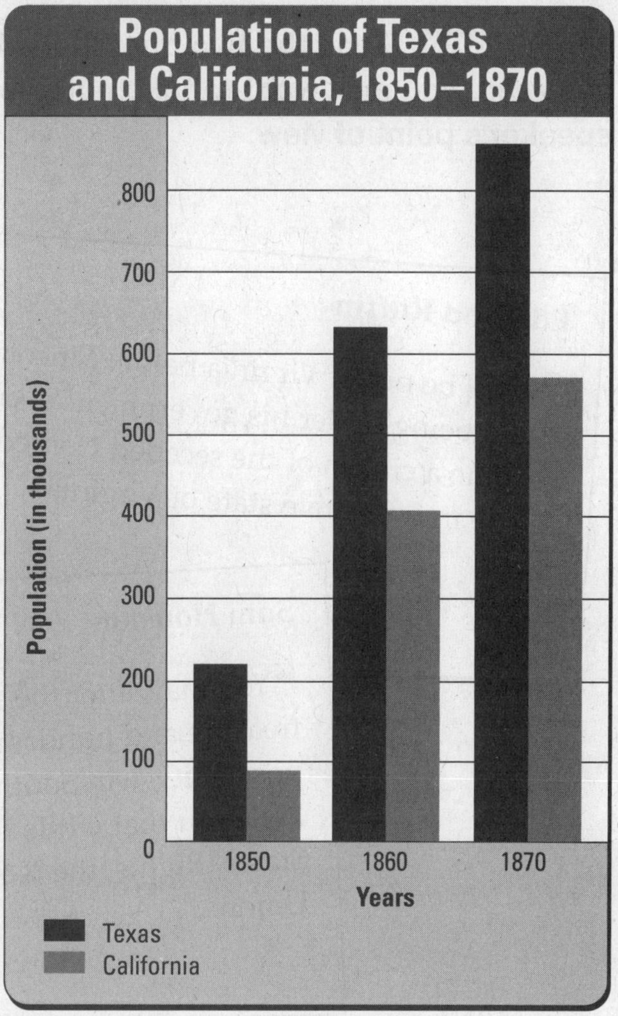

1. About how many people lived in Texas in 1850?

   ____

2. About how many people lived in California in 1850?

   ____

3. Which state had a larger population in 1850, Texas or California?

   ____

4. About how many more people lived in Texas in 1860 than in California?

   ____

   ____

5. Which state had the larger increase in population from 1850 to 1860?

   ____

6. Which state had a population of almost 600 thousand in 1870?

   ____

Name ______________________ Date ____________

The Civil War

When Abraham Lincoln was elected President, many Southerners believed that their way of life would change. In an effort to protect that way of life, they chose to withdraw, or secede, from the Union. Not all Southerners agreed with this action. Many expressed differing points of view.

Directions **Read the two quotations below about Southern secession. As you read, you may want to take notes on a separate sheet of paper about each speaker's point of view.**

Edmund Ruffin

"I will be out of Virginia before Lincoln's inauguration, and so . . . avoid being under his government even for an hour. I, at least, will become a citizen of the seceded Confederate States, and will not again reside in my native state of Virginia. . . ."

Sam Houston

"You may, after the sacrifice of countless millions of treasure and hundreds of thousands of lives, as a bare possibility, win Southern independence . . . But I doubt it. I tell you that while I believe with you in the doctrine of States' Rights, the North is determined to preserve this Union. . . ."

(continued)

 Use after reading Chapter 8, Lesson 2, pages 264–269.

Name ______________________________ Date ______________

Directions **After reading and thinking about the quotations, write an essay in which you compare and contrast the two points of view. Be sure to include why you think these speakers held their different views. Who do you think was the audience for each speaker?**

Name ______________________________ Date ______________

READING SKILLS
Determine Point of View

Directions **Read what two people had to say about slavery. Think about the point of view of each speaker. Then answer the questions.**

A	B
"We provide for our slaves. We give them food. We give them clothing. In return, they give us work. Is this not fair? Who knows if they could find work without us. I love my slaves, and I know they need me. Besides, what is the difference between a slave and anyone else? Like slaves, we too work for our food."	"I believe that slavery is evil. It is evil to own another person. It is evil to take someone's freedom. No matter what the people of the South say, they are doing evil. It is the right of every person in this world to be free. Every person should be able to do what he wants and go where he wants to go."

1. What viewpoint does the speaker of Passage A have? How can you tell?

____

____

2. What statement in Passage A tells you the feelings of the speaker?

____

____

3. What is the viewpoint of the speaker of Passage B? How can you tell?

____

____

4. What statement in Passage B tells you the feelings of the speaker?

____

____

Use after reading Chapter 8, Skill Lesson, pages 270–271.

Name ______________________ Date ____________

Reconstruction

Directions **The passage at the right from General Granger contains words in boldface type. Use context clues to define those words. Match each word in the list below with its definition, and write the correct letter in the blank. Then answer the question that follows.**

> The people of Texas are informed that in **accordance** with a **Proclamation** from the Executive of the United States, all slaves are free. This involves an **absolute equality** of rights and rights of property between former masters and slaves, and the **connection heretofore** existing between former masters and slaves and the connection heretofore existing between them becomes that between employer and **free laborer**. The freedmen are **advised** to remain at their present homes and work for wages. They are informed that they will not be allowed to collect at military posts, and that they will not be supported in **idleness**, either there or elsewhere. By order of
>
> G. Granger
> Major General Commanding

_____ accordance

_____ Proclamation

_____ absolute

_____ equality

_____ connection

_____ heretofore

_____ free laborer

_____ advised

_____ idleness

A. the same rights for all people

B. the act of being joined

C. not occupied or employed

D. someone who can choose where he or she wants to work for pay

E. having no restrictions

F. given advice

G. agreement

H. up to this time

I. an official formal public announcement

In your own words, what is General Granger's order about? ______________________________

____

____

____

____

Name ______________________ Date ______________

War on the Plains

Below are statements from two leaders. Both are asking their followers to fight against enemy forces that greatly outnumber them.

Sam Houston led Texans during the Texas Revolution. He issued these orders to his army in 1836.

Army Orders, 1836

"War is raging on the frontiers. Bejar is surrounded by two thousand of the enemy, . . . The citizens of Texas must rally to the aid of our army, or it will perish. . . . The enemy must be driven from our soil, . . . Independence is declared, it must be maintained. Immediate action, united with valor, alone can achieve the great work. The services of all are forthwith required in the field."

—Sam Houston

In 1867, Satanta, a Kiowa chief, became known as the Orator of the Plains because of the powerful speeches he gave. He made this speech during a meeting with representatives from the United States government.

Speech at Medicine Lodge Creek treaty meeting, 1867

"I love the land and the buffalo. . . . I love to roam over the prairies. . . . A long time ago this land belonged to our fathers, now I see camps of soldiers on the river banks. These soldiers cut down my timber; they kill my buffalo; and when I see that, my heart feels like bursting. . . . This is our country. We have always lived in it. We always had plenty to eat because the land was full of buffalo. We were happy. . . . Then [the enemy] came. . . . We have to protect ourselves. We have to save our country. We have to fight for what is ours."

—Chief Satanta

(continued)

Name ______________________ Date ______________

Directions **Use the quotations from page 84 to help you complete the activities.**

1. Write three ways in which Houston and Satanta express the same thoughts and feelings.

2. Write two ways in which their statements are different.

Name ______________________ Date ____________

Texas and the Civil War

Directions Complete this graphic organizer to help you form opinions from facts related to events about Texas during the Civil War.

FACT →	OPINION
Northerners and Southerners often disagreed about slavery and the power of the national government.	
Abraham Lincoln won the presidential election of 1860, and seven Southern states left the Union. In 1861, Texans voted to secede.	
In 1866, the Texas state government passed Black Codes, which limited the rights of African Americans and led to segregation.	
The United States government wanted Indians to live on reservations so they would be separated from the settlers.	

Use after reading Chapter 8, pages 256–283.

• CHAPTER •

Name ______________________ Date ____________

8 Test Preparation

Directions Read each question and choose the best answer. Then fill in the circle for the answer you have chosen. Be sure to fill in the circle completely.

1. Eli Whitney invented a machine called the—
   - Ⓐ cotton boll.
   - Ⓑ telegraph.
   - Ⓒ cotton gin.
   - Ⓓ telephone.

2. Most Texans wanted to join the Confederate States of America, which was also called the—
   - Ⓕ Lone Star State.
   - Ⓖ Confederacy.
   - Ⓗ Union.
   - Ⓙ United States.

3. What is the name of the state holiday that celebrates the freeing of all slaves in Texas?
   - Ⓐ Juneteenth
   - Ⓑ Reconstruction
   - Ⓒ Black Codes
   - Ⓓ Thirteenth Amendment

4. To rejoin the Union, all Southern states were required by Congress to—
   - Ⓕ allow women to vote in elections.
   - Ⓖ stop shipping cotton to Mexican ports.
   - Ⓗ keep former slaves from voting.
   - Ⓙ write new state constitutions.

5. African American soldiers who fought the Plains Indians were given the nickname—
   - Ⓐ stockade fighters.
   - Ⓑ buffalo soldiers.
   - Ⓒ reservationists.
   - Ⓓ carpetbaggers.

Name ______________________________ Date ______________

The Cattle Kingdom

The Spanish were the ones who introduced cattle in Texas. Both Spanish and Mexican vaqueros taught Texas cattle ranchers and cowhands ranching skills. Soon the language of Texas ranching became flavored with words from Spanish.

Directions **Write the original Spanish word for each of these English words.**

1. lariat ______________
2. lasso ______________
3. rodeo ______________
4. ranch ______________
5. cowhand ______________

Directions **Place the events below in the proper sequence by numbering them from 1 through 6.**

_____ Railroads replaced cattle drives as a faster and easier way to send longhorns to market.

_____ Texas settlers captured wild longhorns and began ranching, mainly in dry regions of South Texas.

_____ The period when cattle ranching was the main business in South and West Texas was known as the Cattle Kingdom.

_____ Cattle drives began in Texas and ended at cities with railroad stations.

_____ The Spanish arrived in Texas, bringing along cattle and keeping them on small ranches or at missions.

_____ Since millions of longhorns roamed Texas, each sold for only $6 to $10 in the state, but a longhorn sold for up to $40 in northern cities.

(continued)

 Use after reading Chapter 9, Lesson 1, pages 300–304.

Name ______________________________ Date ______________

Texas ranch owners created brands that they marked their longhorns with to show ownership. These symbols were usually the rancher's initials in a circle or a design that stood for the name of the ranch. Cattle were rounded up into pens, branded with hot irons, and then herded along cattle trails to market.

Directions **Below are four designs for branding that could be used by Texas ranchers. Design your own brand in the spaces provided. In the last box, think of a name for a ranch and design a brand for it.**

Rocking Chair

Lazy S

Running W

Barbecue

Circle G

Pitchfork

Hat

Rocking Y

____

Name ______________________ Date ______________

Railroads and Industry

Directions **Imagine that you are living in Abilene in the early 1880s, before the railroad arrived. You own a large cattle ranch and want to ship your longhorns to market by railroad. Write a persuasive letter to the Texas and Pacific Railway Company requesting that a railroad be built to run through Abilene.**

Think about:

- How railroads might benefit both communities and businesses in Texas
- How the town of Abilene might change for the better when the railroad arrives

(continued)

 Use after reading Chapter 9, Lesson 2, pages 305–309.

Name ______________________________ Date ______________

When the railroad arrived in Abilene in January 1881, citizens were able to buy a wider variety of goods without leaving their homes. In the past, people were limited to items they could buy locally. Many things could be purchased only in coastal cities. Now, people living in Abilene could place orders through catalogs. Household goods such as sewing machines, cooking stoves, and tools would be delivered by train.

Directions **Design a cover for a catalog to be sent to customers in Abilene. Illustrate the items for sale and describe them. Then, if possible, find out prices for goods in the 1880s, and add a price for each item.**

Name ______________________________ Date ______________

MAP AND GLOBE SKILLS

Use a Time Zone Map

To standardize railroad schedules across the country, time zones were created. This time zone map shows the six time zones across the United States. Because of Earth's rotation, time zones in the east have a later time than those in the west.

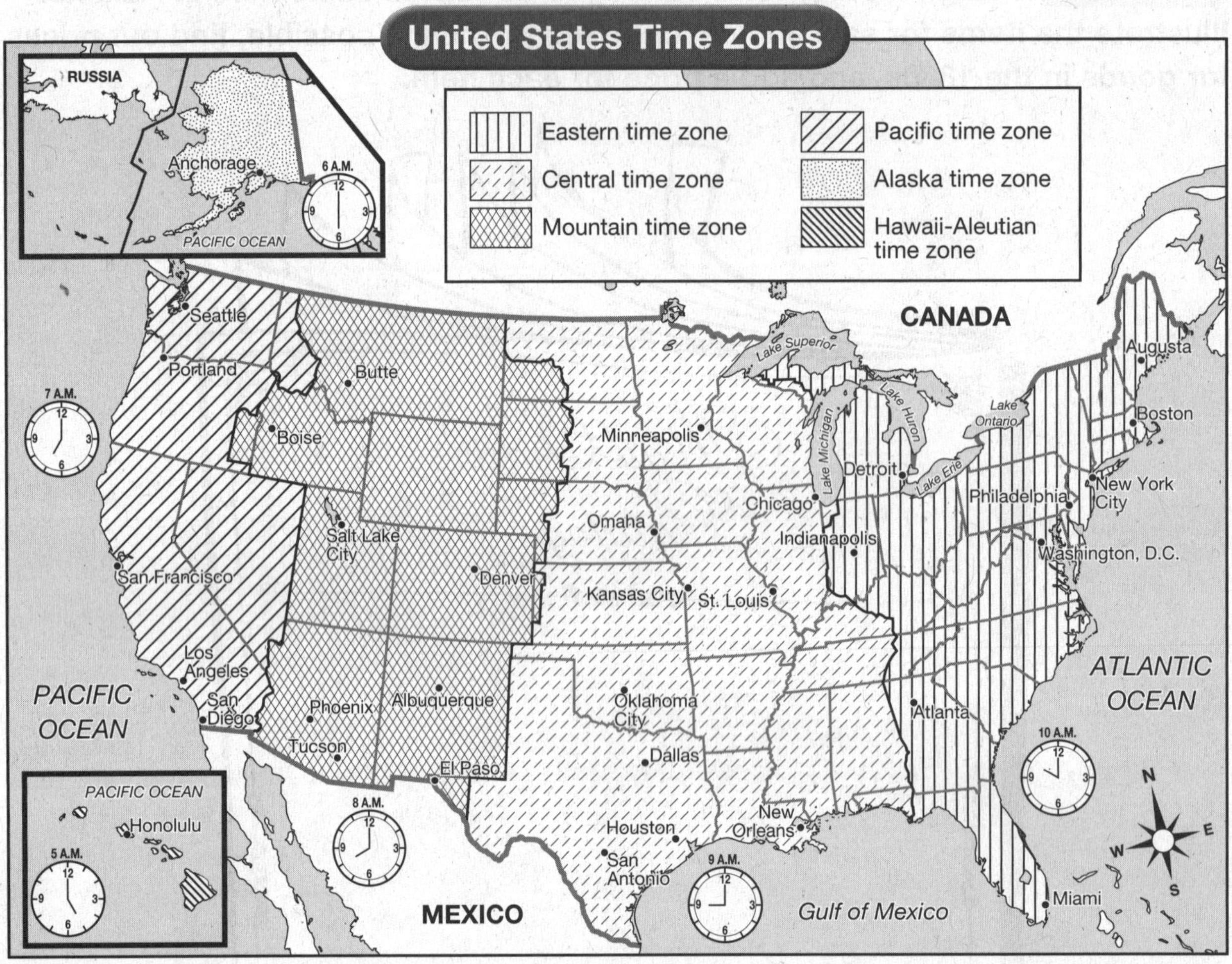

Directions **Use the map to complete the activities.**

1. In which time zone is most of Texas? ______________________________

2. What Texas city is in the mountain time zone? ______________________________

3. Your Alaskan friend asks you to contact her at 10 A.M. If you were in Florida, at what time would you call? ______________________________

4. If you fly from Dallas to Los Angeles, the flight takes three hours. What time will you arrive in Los Angeles if you leave Dallas at 9 A.M.? ______________________________

Use after reading Chapter 9, Skill Lesson, pages 310–311.

Name ______________________ Date ____________

Oil

Directions **Use the clues to complete the word puzzle. The shaded line of letters will spell another word for *oil*.**

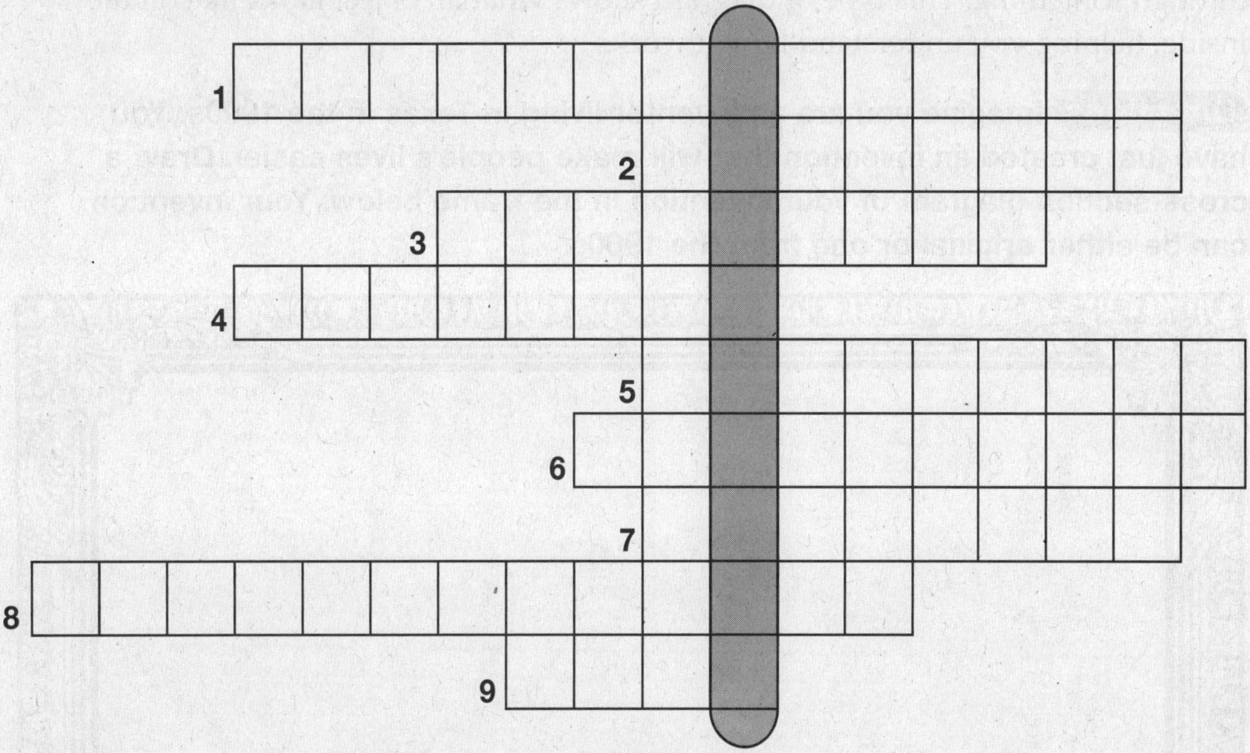

Clues

1. _____ places, such as regions, states, and countries, depend on one another for services and goods.
2. Oil is made into products in a factory called a _____.
3. Texans moved to _____ to find work in the oil fields and to set up new businesses.
4. An _____ makes a living by planning, building, and running machines and structures.
5. The first big oil refinery in Texas was built in _____.
6. A person such as Columbus Marion "Dad" Joiner who searches for new sources of oil is known as a _____.
7. Lumber from East Texas was used to build _____ that supported the well-drilling equipment.
8. To organize and run businesses, _____ need natural, human, and capital resources.
9. The first _____ in the Texas oil industry occurred when people began to drive cars in the early 1900s.

Name ______________________________ Date ______________

CHART AND GRAPH SKILLS

Read a Cross-Section Diagram

A cross-section diagram shows what you would see if you sliced straight through something. This type of diagram shows what an object looks like on the inside, helping you understand how it works.

Directions **Imagine you are an inventor living in Texas in the 1900s. You have just created an invention that will make people's lives easier. Draw a cross-section diagram of your invention in the frame below. Your invention can be either original or one from the 1900s.**

(continued)

Name ______________________ Date ____________

Directions **Now that you've created the invention of the century, you need to encourage people to buy it. Write a persuasive speech that creates interest in your invention. Refer to your cross-section diagram to explain how your invention works. Point out the key features of your invention, showing how this new creation will make life easier for people. Then, deliver your speech to your classmates as you display the cross-section diagram you drew on page 94.**

Name ______________________ Date __________

Texas in a Changing World

Imagine that you are a newspaper reporter in the early 1900s, assigned to interview Christia Adair, the African American suffragist born in Victoria, Texas. This college-educated teacher became one of the few black suffragists in Texas. When she was not admitted to the Texas Equal Suffrage Association because of the color of her skin, Adair did not give up. Nor did she despair when white Texas women got the right to vote in 1918. Adair continued her crusade for equal rights for all Texans.

Directions **Write a list of questions that you would ask Christia Adair in an interview. Include a question about being a good role model for others. Remember to concentrate on the five Ws: who, what, where, when, and why.**

Use after reading Chapter 9, Lesson 4, pages 320–323.

Name ______________________ Date ______________

Texas in World War II

Texans at home played an important role during World War II. Since sugar, butter, meat, gas, and other everyday goods were in short supply, people were given stamp books to ration the amount they could buy. Many Texans grew crops in victory gardens. Some citizens sold war bonds, raising money for the government to help fund World War II. Workers were needed to replace those men who had gone off to war.

Directions **Study the poster from World War II. Then, complete the activities.**

1. What is this poster about? ______________________

2. Why were posters like this one made? ______________________

3. Why was this message important? ______________________

4. What clues does the artist use to get the message across? ______________________

Name ______________________ Date ____________

The Turn of the Century

Directions Complete this graphic organizer to show that you understand the points of view held by different Texans.

SPEAKER AND WORDS	→	POINT OF VIEW
Former Cowhand Cattle drives are impossible. The farmers put up barbed-wire fences, and the railroads can move cattle faster.	→	______________
Farmer The railroad is wonderful! My crops get to market faster. I also receive my farm equipment in much less time.	→	______________
Entrepreneur I moved to Texas to find work. Life in the boomtowns was very difficult. I packed my bags and left.	→	______________
Former Texan The market crashed in 1929, and there was a severe drought. We lost all of our savings. We had to leave Texas.	→	______________
Factory Worker Almost everything Texas produces is needed for World War II. If it weren't for Texas, the war might be lost.	→	______________

Use after reading Chapter 9, pages 298–329.

· CHAPTER ·

9

Name ______________________ Date ______________

Test Preparation

Directions **Read each question and choose the best answer. Then fill in the circle for the answer you have chosen. Be sure to fill in the circle completely.**

1. What did Joseph Glidden invent in 1874?
   Ⓐ the rodeo
   Ⓑ barbed wire
   Ⓒ cattle brands
   Ⓓ spurs

2. The arrival of ______ ended cattle drives in Texas forever.
   Ⓕ railroads
   Ⓖ steamboats
   Ⓗ canals
   Ⓙ automobiles

3. The Texas oil industry experienced a ______ in the early 1900s.
   Ⓐ shortage
   Ⓑ depression
   Ⓒ boom
   Ⓓ stampede

4. Entrepreneurs might use a natural resource such as—
   Ⓕ money.
   Ⓖ buildings.
   Ⓗ machines.
   Ⓙ land.

5. Dust storms and drought plagued a region known as the—
   Ⓐ Great Depression.
   Ⓑ Cattle Kingdom.
   Ⓒ Dust Bowl.
   Ⓓ Chisholm Trail.

Name ______________________ Date ______________

Texas Changes

Directions **Complete this graphic organizer to show that you understand the causes and effects of some of the key events that helped Texas develop into a modern state. Use your textbook to help you.**

CAUSE	EFFECT
During the 1950s, commercial farms began to grow cash crops.	______________________
______________________	In 1950, more people lived in urban areas of Texas than in the countryside.
______________________	Dallas, Fort Worth, Houston, and San Antonio doubled in population.
______________________	The amount of garbage increased, and pollution damaged natural resources.
President John F. Kennedy was assassinated while riding in a Dallas parade.	______________________

(continued)

Use after reading Chapter 10, Lesson 1, pages 334–337.

Name ______________________ Date ______________

Directions **Imagine that your class has decided to create a time capsule. Each student can put in one object that will show people in the future what the time period you live in was like. You can also include a note that describes the object you chose and explains what it says about the time in which you live. The time capsule will be buried in the schoolyard for 50 years. In the space below, write the note that you would include with your object. What might a student think about the object when the time capsule is unearthed fifty years from now?**

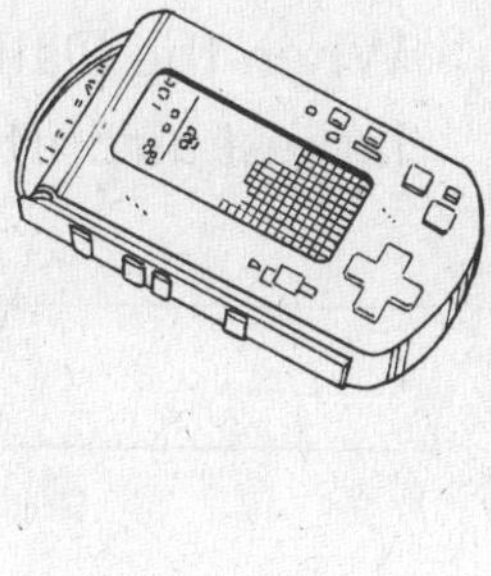

Name ______________________ Date ____________

Changes in Transportation

Directions **Read each passage below. Then summarize the main idea of each passage in the space provided.**

1 Henry Ford revolutionized the automobile industry with changes in manufacturing. As cars cost less to make and prices dropped, demand increased. Larger amounts of oil and gasoline were needed to run the cars. The greater demand for oil and gas helped the economy of Texas cities to grow.

____

____

____

2 Interstate highway systems brought changes to Texas. Some businesses relocated to locations nearer the interstates, hurting small town economies. But the highways also connected suburbs with recreation areas, and visitors helped the Texas economy to grow.

____

____

____

3 After World War I, airplanes mostly delivered mail and goods. By 1928 people could travel by plane to airports in several Texas cities. The Houston Intercontinental Airport opened in 1969, transporting many international visitors. When the Dallas–Fort Worth International Airport opened in 1974, it was the largest airport in the world.

____

____

____

(continued)

Use after reading Chapter 10, Lesson 2, pages 338–343.

Name ______________________________ Date ______________

Directions **Use the clues to complete the word puzzle. The shaded line of letters will spell a popular form of transportation.**

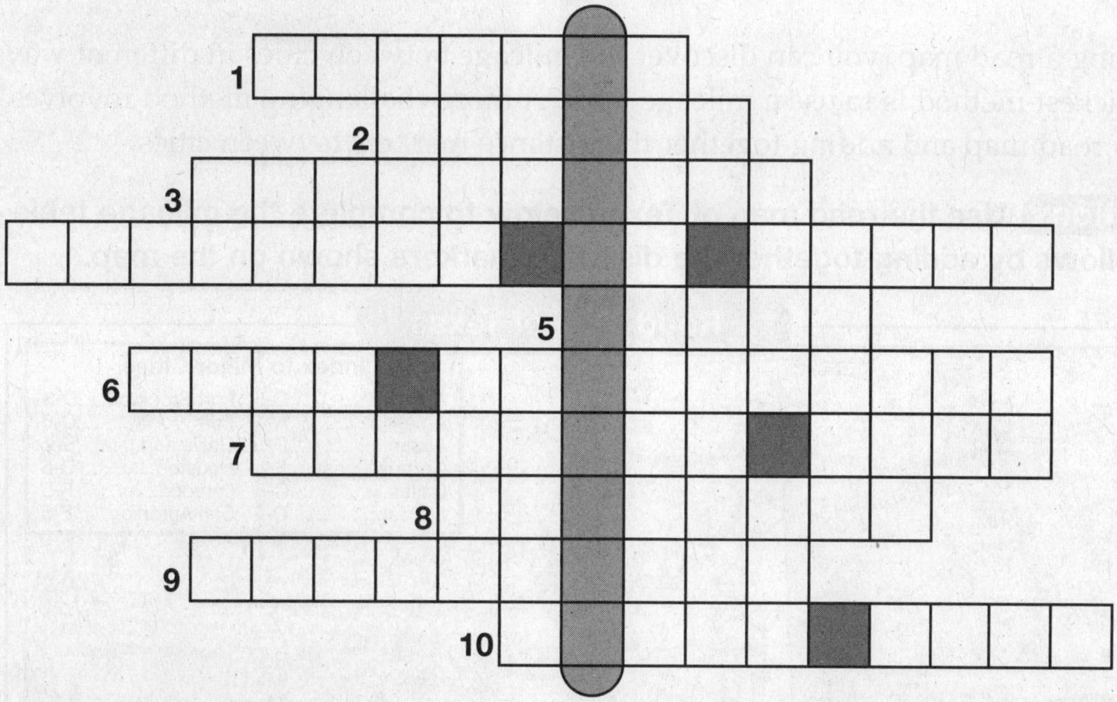

Clues

1. Texas lawmakers set up the State ______ Department in 1917.
2. People who work in a large city can live outside the city in a town or small city called a ______.
3. ______ includes activities people do for fun, such as swimming or hiking.
4. The Ford Company used ______ to build cars by dividing the tasks among a number of workers.
5. In 1916 you would have been able to purchase a ______ T for only $360.
6. Large numbers of items could be manufactured at the same time with ______.
7. On an ______, a product is moved in a line past workers who build it.
8. Not long after the Wright brothers made their first flight, ______ became important to transportation in the United States.
9. If you ______ in something, you work at one kind of job and do it well.
10. In the early 1900s ______ used standardized parts to build his automobiles.

Name ______________________________ Date ______________

MAP AND GLOBE SKILLS

Use a Road Map and Mileage Table

Using a road map, you can discover the mileage between cities in different ways. The quickest method is to use a mileage table. A more challenging method involves using a road map and adding together the distance markers between cities.

Directions **Use the road map of Texas below to complete the mileage table that follows by adding together the distance markers shown on the map.**

Road Map of Texas

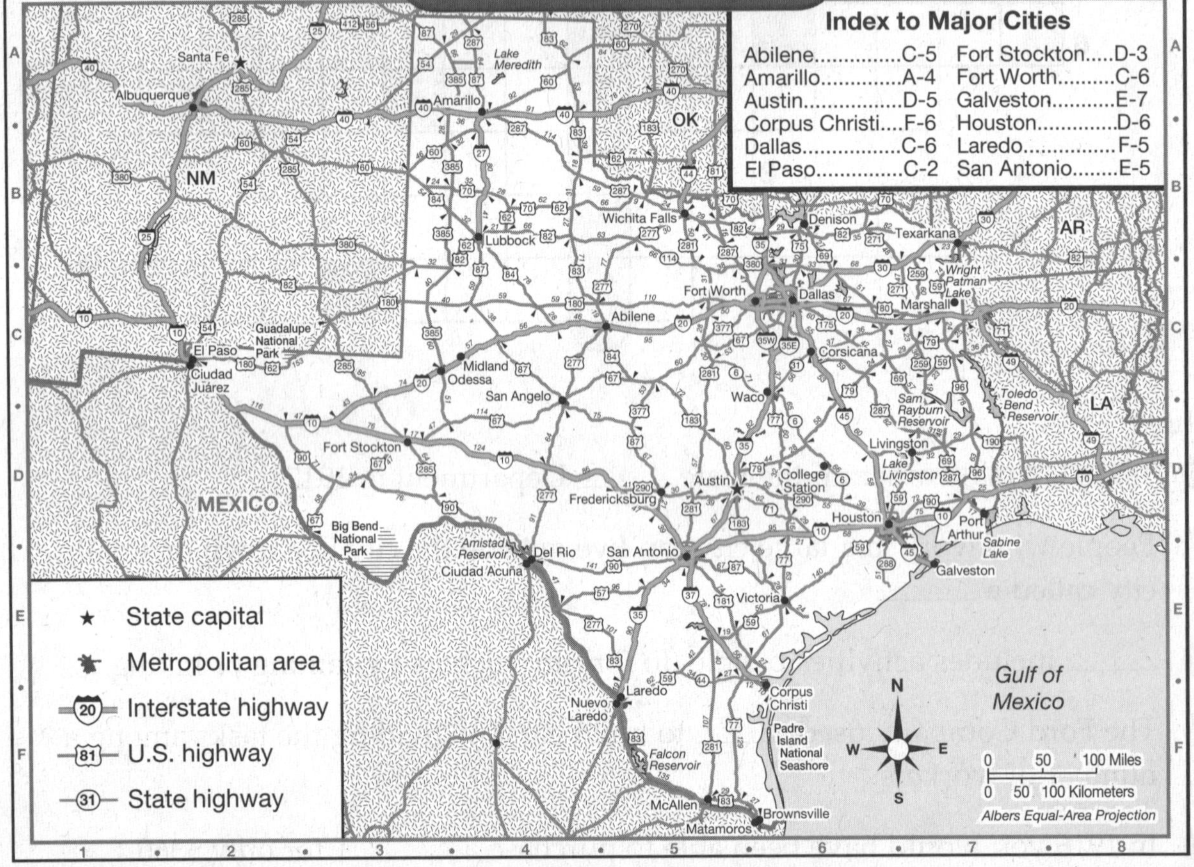

	Amarillo	El Paso	Lubbock	Midland
Amarillo				
El Paso				
Lubbock				
Midland				

(continued)

Use after reading Chapter 10, Skill Lesson, pages 344–345.

Name ______________________ Date ____________

Suppose your local senior citizens center hires you as a bus tour guide. You are in charge of designing a weeklong trip for a group of retired people from Amarillo. They want to go sightseeing at some of the major tourist attractions in Texas.

Directions **Use the road map and the mileage table of Texas on page 104 to answer the following questions.**

1. Beginning from Amarillo, plan a route to your tour's first stop, Lubbock. Here your group is looking forward to seeing the mammoth sculptures at Lubbock Lake Landmark State Historical Park. Which route will get your tour to Lubbock the fastest? How many miles will your route cover?

   ____

   ____

2. Your tour's next stop is Midland, the hometown of President George W. Bush. Which two highways do you need to travel to get there? How far is it?

   ____

   ____

3. Now your tour group wants to take a side trip to El Paso. Here they want to search for golden eagles in Franklin Mountains State Park. Which highways will you take to get there? How many miles is it? ______________________

   ____

4. Now your group wants to return to Amarillo using only roads within Texas. What roads will you take and how many miles will you cover on the way home?

   ____

   ____

Name ______________________________ Date ______________

The Struggle for Civil Rights

Directions **Place the events below in the proper sequence by numbering them from 1 through 7.**

______ Henry B. González became the first Mexican American to be elected to the United States House of Representatives.

______ The Voting Rights Act was passed, banning reading and writing tests and thereby encouraging more minorities to vote.

______ Henry Cisneros became mayor of San Antonio, marking the first time a Hispanic was elected mayor of a large U. S. city.

______ James Farmer helped begin the Congress of Racial Equality to work for African American civil rights.

______ The Civil Rights Act banned segregation in schools and public places, such as hotels and restaurants.

______ Henry B. González was elected to the Texas Senate, becoming the first Mexican American in more than 100 years to hold this post.

______ Barbara Jordan became the first African American to be elected to the Texas Senate in almost 100 years.

 Use after reading Chapter 10, Lesson 3, pages 346–349.

Name ______________________ Date ____________

From Oil to Astronauts

Imagine that President Richard M. Nixon will select one student to blast off with three astronauts on the *Apollo 11* space mission. The student who writes the most convincing letter will board *Apollo 11* at the Kennedy Space Center in Florida on July 16, 1969, with astronauts Neil Armstrong, Edwin E. Aldrin, Jr., and Michael Collins. Four days later, while orbiting the moon, the lunar module *Eagle* will separate from the command module *Columbia*. The student will continue his or her journey with Armstrong and Aldrin aboard the *Eagle* as it becomes the first crewed flight to land upon the moon.

Directions **Write a letter to President Nixon, persuading him to select you to become one of the first people to walk on the moon. Why do you want to make this journey? What will you do for the 2 hours and 32 minutes you spend on the moon? What photographs will you take?**

Name ______________________ Date ______________

READING SKILLS

Predict a Likely Outcome

Each December 31, as the year ends, people often make predictions about what will happen in the new year or beyond. New ideas, discoveries, and technologies are often part of these predictions. For example, in 1949 someone might have predicted that he or she would watch the news on television in the 1950s.

Directions At the dawn of the new millennium, many writers examined predictions that were made in the twentieth century that proved to be false. Read the following predictions and then explain why each is incorrect.

1. "I think there is a world market for about five computers." —Thomas J. Watson, IBM chief (1943)

2. "People will soon get tired of staring at a plywood box every night." —Darryl F. Zanuck, film producer, on the future of television (1946)

3. "The actual building of roads devoted to motor cars is not for the near future, in spite of many rumors to that effect." —*Harper's Weekly,* August 2, 1902

Directions Now write your own prediction for the coming year about a new technology, idea, or discovery that will change life in Texas. Write your prediction on a separate sheet of paper and share it with your classmates.

Use after reading Chapter 10, Skill Lesson, page 355.

Name ______________________ Date ____________

The Latter Twentieth Century

Directions Complete this graphic organizer to show that you can draw conclusions about Texas in the latter part of the twentieth century.

EVIDENCE		CONCLUSION
Many cities grew after World War II. In 1948, Houston was the fastest-growing city in the United States.	→	
KNOWLEDGE		
When the population of a city grows, more services are needed.	→	

EVIDENCE		CONCLUSION
Mass production made it easier to produce automobiles and for people to afford them.	→	
KNOWLEDGE		
	→	

EVIDENCE		CONCLUSION
Starting in the 1950s, many people in the United States wanted equal treatment for all people.	→	
KNOWLEDGE		
	→	

EVIDENCE		CONCLUSION
In the 1980s, other countries began selling more of their oil in the United States.	→	
KNOWLEDGE		
	→	

• CHAPTER •

10

Name ______________________________ Date ______________

Test Preparation

Directions **Read each question and choose the best answer. Then fill in the circle for the answer you have chosen. Be sure to fill in the circle completely.**

1. The thirty-sixth President, ______, came from Stonewall, Texas.
   - Ⓐ Christia Adair
   - Ⓑ Patillo Higgins
   - Ⓒ Dwight Eisenhower
   - Ⓓ Lyndon B. Johnson

2. Texas ports lead all other states in shipping—
   - Ⓕ agricultural products.
   - Ⓖ passengers.
   - Ⓗ chemicals and oil.
   - Ⓙ mail and automobiles.

3. The Civil Rights Act of 1964 banned—
   - Ⓐ minorities.
   - Ⓑ segregation.
   - Ⓒ equal rights.
   - Ⓓ voting.

4. The end to the growth of the Texas oil industry in the 1980s was called—
   - Ⓕ a bust.
   - Ⓖ a demand.
   - Ⓗ a boom.
   - Ⓙ a prediction.

5. Where did NASA open a new headquarters to train astronauts?
   - Ⓐ Houston
   - Ⓑ Cape Canaveral
   - Ⓒ San Antonio
   - Ⓓ Denison

Use after reading Chapter 10, pages 332–355.

Name ____________________ Date ____________

Local Governments in Texas

Directions **Choose three leaders of your community's government to learn more about. Complete this chart with information you find in the library, in the newspaper, or on the Internet.**

Name of My Community: ____________________

Leader 1	Title and Job Description	Leadership Qualities
Leader 2	**Title and Job Description**	**Leadership Qualities**
Leader 3	**Title and Job Description**	**Leadership Qualities**

Use after reading Chapter 11, Lesson 1, pages 370–374.

Name ______________________ Date ______________

Texas State Government

The Texas state government is composed of three parts: the legislative branch, the executive branch, and the judicial branch. Each branch performs a different function, but all three work together to complement one another. One branch creates the laws, the second makes sure the laws are observed, and the third determines whether the laws are fair.

Directions **The chart below shows the three branches of the Texas state government. Complete the chart by filling in the empty boxes beneath the leaders' titles with two responsibilities that they perform.**

The Three Branches of the Texas State Government

Legislative Branch	Executive Branch	Judicial Branch
Makes state laws.	Sees that the laws are carried out.	Decides whether the laws are fair and constitutional.
Senators and Representatives	**Governor of Texas**	**Supreme Court Justices**
______________________	______________________	______________________

(continued)

Use after reading Chapter 11, Lesson 2, pages 375–379.

Name ______________________________ Date ______________

Directions **Write each of these terms next to the sentence below that tells about it.**

appeal	judicial branch	legislative branch
bills	justices	veto
executive branch		

1. ______________ This branch of government consists of two parts—the Senate and the House of Representatives, both of which make state laws.

2. ______________ After ordering an emergency meeting of the legislature, the governor can do this to bills, thereby stopping them from becoming laws.

3. ______________ Elected by Texas voters, these eight people along with the Chief Justice make up the Supreme Court.

4. ______________ These plans for new laws, also known by this name, can help protect citizens' lives, freedoms, and property.

5. ______________ The head of this branch is the governor of Texas, who serves a four-year term after being elected by voters.

6. ______________ Citizens can do this by requesting another trial if they want to change a court decision.

7. ______________ Courts and judges make up this branch, which ensures that Texas laws are fair.

LEGISLATIVE BRANCH	EXECUTIVE BRANCH	JUDICIAL BRANCH

Texas House of Representatives and Texas Senate	Governor and State Agencies	Courts

Name ______________________ Date ______________

CHART AND GRAPH SKILLS

Read a Flow Chart

A flow chart helps you to visualize information. When the information is displayed step-by-step in a drawing, it is often easier to understand. Here's an example of a flow chart describing how to bathe a dog.

Bathing a Dog

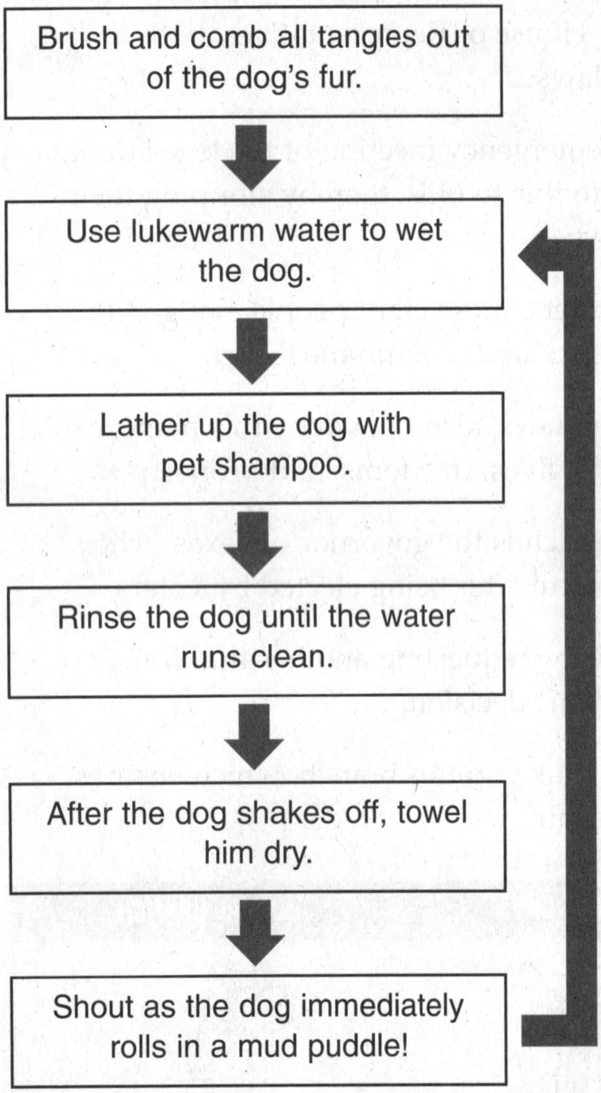

Directions **Now, come up with your own activity, such as washing a car or baking a birthday cake. Draw a flow chart of the activity in the right-hand column. First, break the activity down into steps. Use one sentence to describe each step. Put each step in a box, and then draw an arrow linking it to the next step. Your chart will flow from top to bottom. Remember to give your flow chart a title.**

Name ______________________________ Date ______________

Texas and the National Government

Directions **Play this "Who Am I?" game by matching the names of Texans in the national government with their descriptions. Draw a line to connect the name of each person in the right column with his or her description in the left column.**

1. After President John F. Kennedy's death in 1963, I served as the thirty-sixth President. The following year, I was elected President.
2. I became the first woman senator from Texas. Based in Dallas, I was elected to the United States Senate in 1993.
3. During World War II, I served as general in charge of troops in Europe. When I was elected President in 1952, I helped set up the interstate highway system.
4. I became Speaker of the United States House of Representatives in 1940.
5. I became the first woman to serve on the Supreme Court. Born in El Paso, I was appointed to my position by President Ronald Reagan in 1981.
6. My father was the forty-first President of the United States. I followed in his footsteps, becoming the forty-third President in 2001.
7. Born in Houston, I became the first African American woman to win a seat in the Texas Senate. In 1972, I was elected to the United States House of Representatives.

Sandra Day O'Connor

George W. Bush

Dwight D. Eisenhower

Kay Bailey Hutchison

Barbara Jordan

Sam Rayburn

Lyndon Baines Johnson

Name ______________________ Date ____________

Texas Citizenship

Directions **Fill in the missing information about citizenship.**

1. Many Texas citizens are active in ______________________ groups, such as those working to save historical monuments and buildings.

2. In order to become a ______________________, immigrants must first live in the United States for at least five years.

3. Fifteen years after immigrating from ______________________ to El Paso, Cleofas Calleros became a United States citizen and then devoted his life to helping other immigrants.

4. According to the United States ______________________ "all persons born or naturalized in the United States . . . are citizens of the United States and of the State wherein they reside."

5. Once citizens reach the age of ______________________, they are given the right to vote.

6. Citizens promise their loyalty to the United States when they say the Pledge of ______________________.

7. Citizens can ______________________ to vote by filling out an application.

8. Texas laws state that it is a citizen's ______________________ to obey laws, pay taxes, and be loyal to the United States.

9. September 17 is both ______________________ Day and the date on which the United States Constitution was signed in 1787.

10. Only United States citizens can vote, be members of trial ______________________, and hold public office.

(continued)

Use after reading Chapter 11, Lesson 4, pages 389–393.

Name ________________________________ Date ______________

Use Your Interests to Serve Your Community

Across the nation people help others in their communities by volunteering. There are many opportunities for people of all ages to volunteer. People collect food from neighbors to stock food banks and homeless shelters, pick up litter along rivers and streams, and raise money to help disaster victims. Others volunteer at animal shelters, nursing homes, and schools. People also help their neighbors by providing transportation, helping with household chores, cooking meals, or simply keeping them company. Volunteer opportunities are limited only by one's imagination!

Directions Think of things you like to do that might also help somebody else. List some of these things in the column on the left below. Next to each item, on the right, list ways you could use that interest or talent as a volunteer. You might find a list of volunteer groups in your local newspaper.

Things I Like to Do	Ways I Can Help

Name ______________________________ Date ______________

CITIZENSHIP SKILLS

Act as a Responsible Citizen

You can make a difference in your school and your community by acting as a responsible citizen. What does a responsible citizen do? He or she is aware of local events and problems that affect the community. Responsible citizens learn what can be done to solve problems and take action to make things better.

Directions **As a responsible citizen, what can you do to help your class and your school? Draw a poster asking your classmates to elect you class president. Include a problem that you think should be solved. For example, your classmates might want more books added to the school library. Or maybe you think an after-school reading program would help you and your classmates. As responsible citizens, why should your classmates elect you? Think about answers to this question as you draw your poster.**

Name ______________________ Date ____________

Government in Texas

Directions **Complete this graphic organizer with details that categorize ideas about government and citizenship in Texas.**

LOCAL GOVERNMENT IN TEXAS

City Governments ____________________

____

____

County Governments ____________________

____

____

Special Districts ____________________

____

____

TEXAS STATE GOVERNMENT

Legislative Branch ____________________

____

____

Executive Branch ____________________

____

____

Judicial Branch ____________________

____

____

TEXAS AND THE NATIONAL GOVERNMENT

United States Government ____________________

____

____

Texans in the National Government

____

____

____

____

____

TEXAS CITIZENSHIP

Rights of Citizens ____________________

____

____

Responsibilities of Citizens ____________________

____

____

____

____

____

CHAPTER 11

Name ______________________ Date ____________

Test Preparation

Directions **Read each question and choose the best answer. Then fill in the circle for the answer you have chosen. Be sure to fill in the circle completely.**

1. In Texas state government, laws are made by the—
   - Ⓐ judicial branch.
   - Ⓑ executive branch.
   - Ⓒ citizens.
   - Ⓓ legislative branch.

2. A duty of the Texas governor is to—
   - Ⓕ appoint senators to the Senate.
   - Ⓖ make state tax laws.
   - Ⓗ call out the Texas National Guard if necessary.
   - Ⓙ vote on bills.

3. Who replaced Lyndon Johnson as Texas senator?
   - Ⓐ John Tower
   - Ⓑ Sandra Day O'Connor
   - Ⓒ George Bush
   - Ⓓ Barbara Jordan

4. Citizens must ______ before they can vote.
   - Ⓕ appeal
   - Ⓖ register
   - Ⓗ veto
   - Ⓙ serve

5. After receiving the Purple Heart medal, Cleofas Calleros became ______ in June of 1918.
   - Ⓐ an immigrant
   - Ⓑ city manager
   - Ⓒ Texas governor
   - Ⓓ a naturalized citizen

Use after reading Chapter 11, pages 368–395.

Name ______________________________ Date ______________

A Free Enterprise Economy

Directions **Complete each sentence by writing a word in the blank. Then write the same word in the space with the same number below. Finally, read down to find the answer to this riddle: I can be yellow corn, and sparkling gold, and a tumbling river, and fresh-cut lumber. What am I? a ______________**

1. A radio that is made in Japan and sold in Texas is an example of an ______________.
2. A Texas farmer sells wheat to Russia. That is an example of an ______________.
3. Someone who comes to see Texas and stays in a hotel is helping the business of ______________.
4. A store owner sells a bicycle and has money left over after paying expenses. That money is called ______________.
5. When you pay money to have a haircut, you are a ______________.
6. Free ______________ means that people own and run their own businesses.
7. When two companies are trying to get people to buy similar products, they are in ______________.
8. A resource that can be made again and again is a ______________ resource.

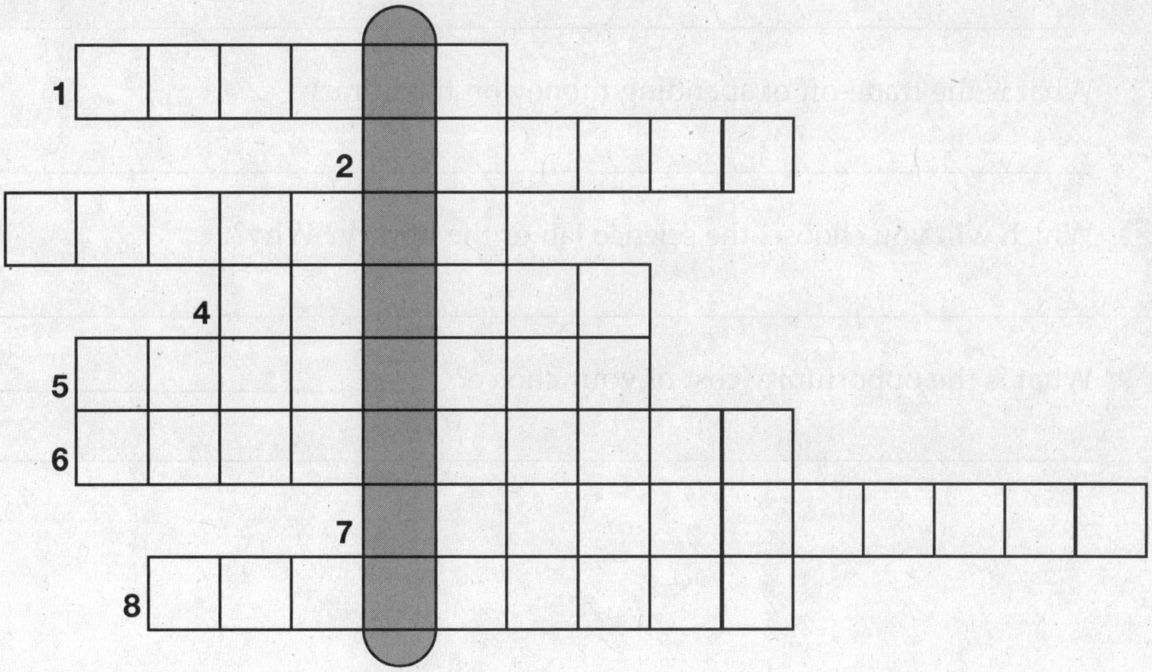

Name ______________________ Date ______________

CITIZENSHIP SKILLS

Make Economic Choices

Directions The number of students in your school has increased, so the science lab and the library are now used as classrooms. Your school has enough money to build either a science lab or a library. Answer the questions below to help your school decide what to do. Be sure to think about the trade-offs.

1. What are the reasons to spend the money on the science lab?

____

____

What is the trade-off of spending money on the science lab?

____

2. What are the reasons to spend the money on a library? ______________________

____

____

What is the trade-off of spending money on the library?

____

3. Which will you choose, the science lab or the library? Why?

____

4. What is the opportunity cost of your choice? ______________________

____

Use after reading Chapter 12, Skill Lesson, pages 404–405.

Name ____________________ Date ____________

Growth and the Environment

Directions **The boxes below show some of the causes and effects of how growth in Texas affected the environment. Fill in the boxes with the missing cause or effect.**

CAUSE	EFFECT
People moved to Texas, and industries grew. That meant that many areas where plants and animals lived were cleared for factories and homes.	____________________
____________________	If the chemicals and fertilizers run off into rivers, the water becomes polluted.
People recycle by using materials again.	____________________
____________________	Soil conservation stops soil erosion on farms and ranches.
Large areas of Texas are set aside as state and national parks.	____________________

Name ______________________ Date ______________

MAP AND GLOBE SKILLS

Read a Population Map

This map of Mexico shows Mexico's population density per square mile.

Population of Mexico

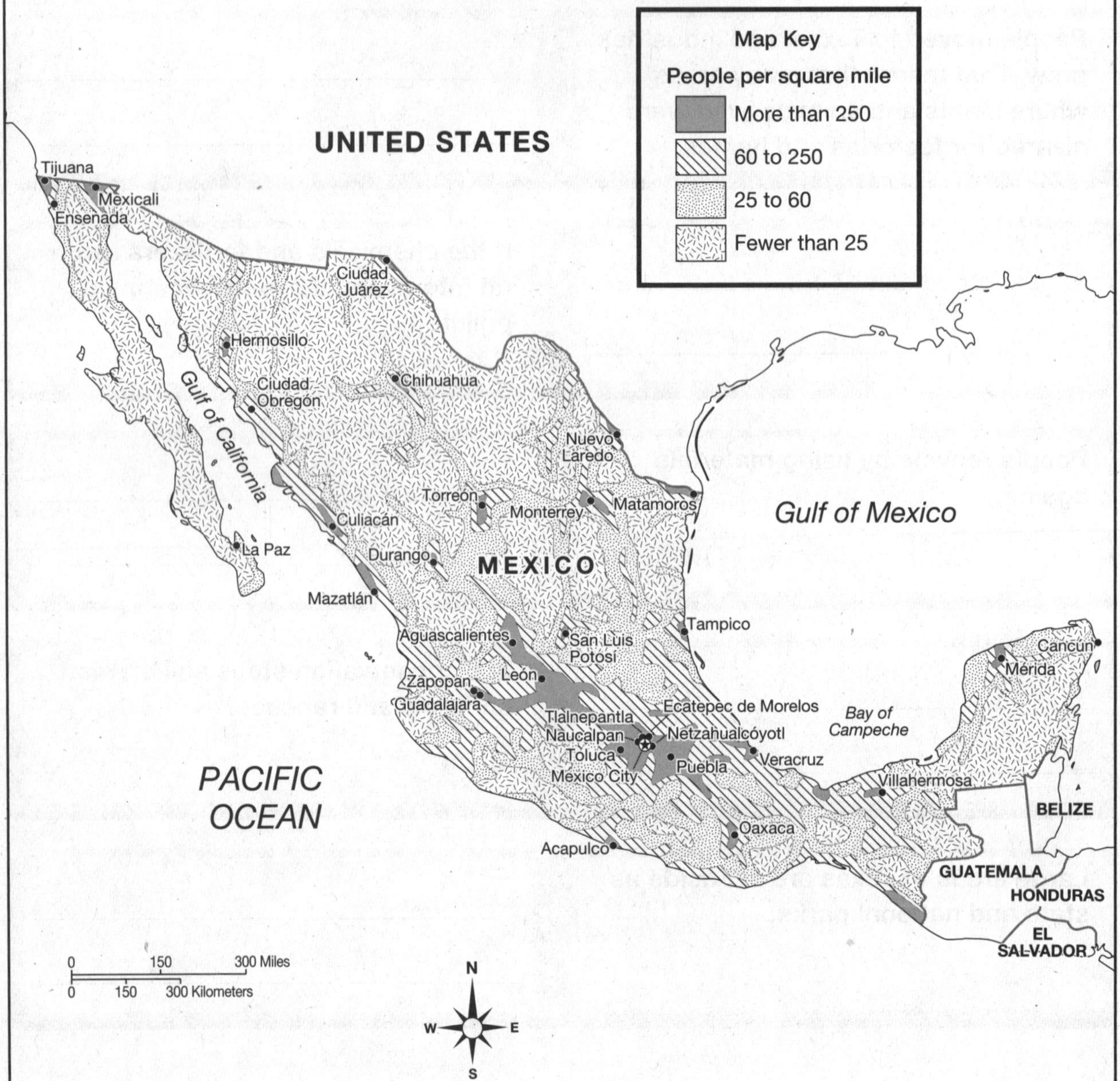

(continued)

 Use after reading Chapter 12, Skill Lesson, pages 410–411.

Name ______________________ Date ____________

Directions **Use the population density map of Mexico on page 124 to answer these questions.**

1. What is the lowest population density on the map?

   ____

2. What is the population density of the city of León?

   ____

3. Which settlement along the Gulf of California has the greater population density, La Paz or Ciudad Obregón? ______________________

4. Where are there more densely populated cities, near the Gulf of Mexico or near the Pacific Ocean? ______________________

5. Where is the least crowded part of Mexico? ______________________

   ____

6. What could explain why the area around Chihuahua has so few people compared to Mexico City? ______________________

   ____

   ____

   ____

7. How might population density mean a different kind of life for someone who lives in Mexico City as opposed to someone who lives in Nuevo Laredo?

   ____

   ____

   ____

   ____

Name ______________________________ Date ______________

Texan Pride

Many people come to Texas to experience the culture. Imagine that you are one of them. You are on a trip through Texas to visit relatives, and you are writing postcards to a friend back home in Kansas.

On the first day, you went to a Mexican festival, ate tacos and other Mexican food, and listened to mariachi music.

Directions On this postcard, write about your experience at the festival. Describe what you saw, what you ate, and what you did.

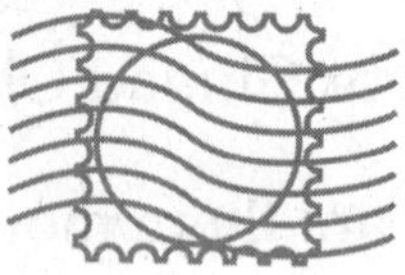

The next day, you went to the Texas State Fair.

Directions On this postcard, describe your trip to the state fair. Write about what you did, saw, heard, and ate at the fair.

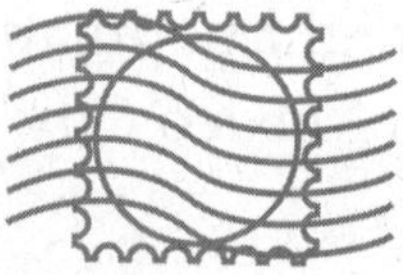

(continued)

Name ______________________ Date ______________

The third day, you went to a party at a cousin's elementary school. The school has students from many of Texas's immigrant and ethnic groups. It was an international party, and everyone brought a dish from his or her culture. Many people brought instruments and sang or played music from their cultures.

Directions **On this postcard, write about what happened at the party. Tell your friend about the many different people you met and where their ancestors were from. Describe the food you ate or the music you listened to.**

The day before you left Texas, you went to a professional sports event.

Directions **On this postcard, tell about the game. Describe what happened, what the sport was, and how the team got its name, if you can. Then tell your friend what your overall impression of Texas is.**

Name ______________________________ Date ______________

Texas Tomorrow

Directions **The chart below lists some inventions. Fill in the chart to tell more about them and their importance to Texas.**

Technology	What is it?	When was it first used?	What is the use of this technology?
telegraph 	device that uses electricity to send messages in code	1854	
telephone 	device that allows voices to be spoken and heard over wires	1879	
space technology 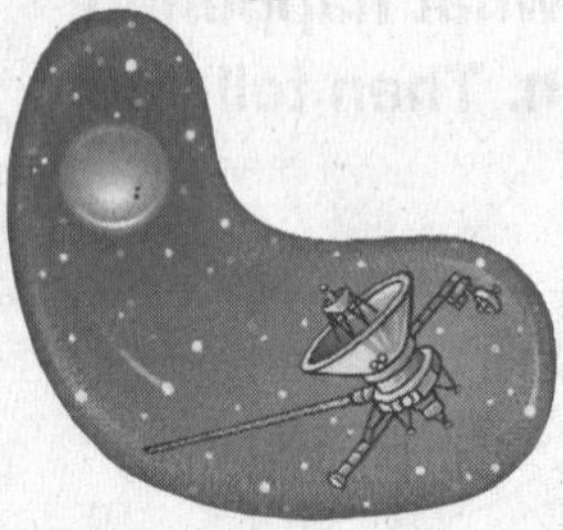	smoke detectors, scratch-resistant eyeglasses, cordless power tools, satellites	1960s	
Internet 	network that links computers	last few years	

 Use after reading Chapter 12, Lesson 4, pages 416–419.

Name ______________________ Date ____________

Texas, the United States, and the World

Directions Complete this graphic organizer to help you list events and the outcomes of these events that affect Texas, the United States, and the world.

EVENT	→	OUTCOME
Lesson 1: A Free Enterprise Economy ______ ______ ______	→	**Outcome:** ______ ______ ______
Lesson 2: Growth and the Environment ______ ______ ______	→	**Outcome:** ______ ______ ______
Lesson 3: Texan Pride ______ ______ ______	→	**Outcome:** ______ ______ ______
Lesson 4: Texas Tomorrow ______ ______ ______	→	**Outcome:** ______ ______ ______

Use after reading Chapter 12, pages 398–419.

CHAPTER 12

Name ______________________ Date ______________

Test Preparation

Directions **Read each question and choose the best answer. Then fill in the circle for the answer you have chosen. Be sure to fill in the circle completely.**

1. The industry that provides services to travelers who visit a place is called—
   - Ⓐ free enterprise.
   - Ⓑ competition.
   - Ⓒ tourism.
   - Ⓓ resources.

2. Goods shipped by Texas to another state or country to be sold are known as—
   - Ⓕ exports.
   - Ⓖ consumers.
   - Ⓗ imports.
   - Ⓙ reports.

3. Some wilderness areas were lost when people and industries—
   - Ⓐ recycled garbage.
   - Ⓑ conserved resources.
   - Ⓒ moved to Texas.
   - Ⓓ protected endangered animals.

4. Conjunto and mariachi are—
   - Ⓕ Texas festivals.
   - Ⓖ favorite Texas foods.
   - Ⓗ sports Texans like to watch.
   - Ⓙ types of music heard in Texas.

5. What is the name of a region of mild climate that stretches from the southeastern United States through the Southwest?
   - Ⓐ Black Gold
   - Ⓑ Sun Belt
   - Ⓒ Fair Park
   - Ⓓ Padre Island National Seashore

Use after reading Chapter 12, pages 398–419.